CATCH PIKE

THE ANGLING TIMES LIBRARY

CATCH PIKE

WITH

JOHN WILSON

Boxtree

in association with
ANGLING TIMES

First published in the UK 1991
by Boxtree Limited, 36 Tavistock Street,
London WC2E 7PB

1 3 5 7 9 10 8 6 4 2

Angling Times is a weekly newspaper produced by EMAP
Publishing Limited, Bretton, Peterborough. Established in
1953, it is Britain's biggest selling weekly fishing publica-
tion. Every week it offers authoritative expert news, views
and advice on all aspects of coarse, sea and game fishing.
On sale every Wednesday.

Illustrations by David Batten
Cover design by Dave Goodman/Millions Design
Design by Peter Ward

Set in 10/13pt Linotron Bembo
Typeset by Cambrian Typesetters, Frimley
Colour origination by Fotographics, Hong Kong
Printed and bound in the UK by Richard Clay, Bungay

A catalogue record for this book is available
from the British Library.

ISBN 1 85283 126 X

CONTENTS

ACKNOWLEDGEMENTS

NO angling writer can produce a book without considerable help from others. Allow me therefore to thank the editing and design team, the mates who leave their own fishing to photograph me, and a very special thank you to good friend Dave Batten who has made such a fine job of the line drawings.

John Wilson
Great Witchingham
1991

INTRODUCTION

THE pike has always been popular among freshwater anglers due to its voraciousness, the folklore and mystery that surrounds its predatory 'dog eat dog' lifestyle, and because after carp, pike provide by far the best opportunity of coming to grips with something big, say 10 lb or more. And of course, being long, even a 10 lb pike does, with its dental armoury, appear quite some adversary.

There is a distinct chance on most waters of even inexperienced pike anglers latching on to that magical 20-pounder. And such a fish, while it does not necessarily fight with the same speed or acrobatic agility as smaller fish, does look immensely impressive. So there are indeed rich rewards for those who brave winter weather in pursuit of *Esox lucius*; although to be fair, pike actually fight considerably harder and with more aggression during the warmer months when their metabolic rate is at its highest,

There is no doubt that static deadbaits account for pike of a higher than average size. This Broadland brace, together weighing almost 50 lb, accepted float-fished half herrings to the rod of John's regular fishing companion, Doug Allen of Norwich.

than they do in the low temperatures of winter. Warm-
weather sport with this predator is just waiting to be
enjoyed by a majority of pike fishermen, who at present
put optimum weight before excitement.

Working artificial lures through lily-pads in July, for
instance, may lose out to the more traditional early-season
pursuit of bream, tench or carp, but provides exciting
sport for anyone willing to try it.

The emphasis of this book, and my own pike fishing, is
on catching pike by a number of interesting techniques,
from many different fisheries, and from both boat and
bank. For example, the static deadbait is out-and-away the
most effective method of contacting larger-than-average
pike, but until a run occurs it is a most inactive technique
that produces fish more through patience than opportunism.
On the other hand, methods such as wandering along the
bank wobbling small deadbaits, or retrieving artificial
lures, catch through mobility, impatience and an ability to
read the water, thus working the bait through areas where
pike are most likely to be lying – the choice of method is
yours.

CHAPTER ONE

THE
SPECIES

PIKE
(Esox lucius)

Not only is the pike the ultimate predator, one might also
say it is the ultimate survivor. From fossil remains it would
appear that the pike has been around longer than all other
freshwater species in the British Isles.

When my good friend, Dave Green, started Bure Valley
Trout Fisheries near Aylsham in North Norfolk a few
years back and the aggregate diggers moved in to remove
the rich seam of minerals, geologists from both Cromer
and Norwich museums soon became interested in the
quality of the animal fossil remains that were uncovered.
These were creatures which had lived during the Ipswichian
interglacial period around 120,000 years ago, and high on
the list of fish fossils was none other than *Esox lucius*, the
very same pike for which we fish today.

In his excellent book *Pike*, Fred Buller reveals that the
earliest pike fossils to be found in Britain, again in my
home county of Norfolk, came from the Cromer Forest
beds at West Runton. This land has long since been
reclaimed by the sea, but the fossil stumps of trees can still
be seen at exceptionally low tides. And the approximate
time-scale for this particular interglacial period, when sea
levels were substantially lower than they are today (which
accounts for Cromer Forest now being part of the seabed),
is half a million years ago. Fred Buller's painstaking,
monumental research also revealed *Esox lepidotus*, an
ancient pike little different to the one we catch today. The
fossil remains, found in Germany, date back a staggering
20 million years.

Why has the pike survived for many millions of years
and through numerous ice ages when species like the
burbot, for instance, common in East Anglia at the turn of

Although anglers feel delighted at having deceived the pike, it is indeed a sobering thought that this same predator has survived in British freshwaters for at least half a million years.

the century, have now become extinct? The burbot's disappearance could well be attributed to the vast quantities of chemicals now present in our freshwaters, because in Canada and Scandinavian countries like Sweden, where the waters are still clear, pure and sweet, burbot are extremely common and form part of the food source of local communities.

Despite what mother nature and civilization throws at the pike, however, it overcomes all. It is the ultimate predatory survivor, forever adapting to local conditions and perfectly equipped for hunting out its prey. Locked in an evolutionary time warp, it will undoubtedly remain long after the human race has gone and the pages of this book have disintegrated into fine powder.

Physically the pike is exceptionally well equipped. The pike lacks the top speed of trout, but its acceleration off the blocks is legendary. From a standing start the thrust from its large, powerful tail instantly propels the pike forwards (the dorsal fin is set far back to assist this) at incredible speed. Prey fish do escape, however, because sometimes the pike's timing is out and it misses, in spite of its monstrously large jaws. Nevertheless, it catches more

The pike's ferocity is legendary. They attack and swallow waterbirds such as dab chicks, moorhens and coots with more regularity than anglers may realize. A fully grown mallard would easily slip between this pike's enormous jaws.

often than not. The pike is also able to swallow almost anything – in fur, feather or scales – little smaller than itself.

Occasionally the pike takes on more than it can chew and chokes to death in the process. For example, on the Norfolk Broads, where eels are particularly plentiful in the thick layers of organic silt, it commonly happens that a pike is caught on a large deadbait and is found to have the tail end of a partly digested eel protruding from its jaws. It is understandable that, in a flash of aggression, a pike might make a reflex hit on a spinner or livebait that passes close by while it is digesting a reasonably-sized eel. But deliberately to locate and suck up a large static deadbait from the bottom when its jaws and throat are already full can surely only be attributed to greed.

There have been occasional reports in the angling press of pike, and not monsters at that, taking on considerably

more than they bargained for. An example is the 14 lb pike
that in heavily coloured water grabbed hold of a soft and
furry meal swimming slowly along 2 ft under the surface
in an agitated fashion. It turned out to be a front paw of a
100 lb German Shepherd having a swim alongside a boat
in which sat his master. This perfectly true story appeared
in *Angling Times* some years back, and there have since
been numerous lesser attacks on very much smaller dogs.
After all, when a pike looks up for instance at a Jack Russell
terrier paddling along, it sees a potential meal that covers
little more surface area than a mallard. The pike which
grabbed the German Shepherd would have assumed that
the paw (which was all it could have seen in such muddy
water) was a vole, mole or rat, all of which are eaten by
pike, as are all kinds of water birds – dab chicks,
moorhens, coots, mallards, etc. A big pike is quite capable
of swallowing even adult birds.

For many years I was rather sceptical about stories of
coots and ducks disappearing; ducklings yes, because
beneath the fluff they are no larger than the deadbaits we
use for catching pike every weekend. But then it happened
before my very eyes. I was out on a particularly cold,
frosty morning with the lure rod working a Big S plug
along a deep gully running parallel with the margins on a
local gravel pit. The surface was completely still and like a
sheet of glass. A few coots were dotted here and there,
and when from the corner of one eye I suddenly noticed a
large swirl appear on the surface to my left, I assumed it to
be a diving coot, but nothing came up. With the water so
cold and clear the idea of a pike striking on the surface
seemed strange. A few minutes later I arrived opposite the
spot and cranked the plug down through the deep,
incredibly clear water.

Half-way through the retrieve the rod buckled over and
I was fast into a lively, double-figure pike of around 18 lb.
I distinctly remember marvelling at its beautiful markings,
which could be clearly seen in the bright sunshine, even
deep down. Then the pike hit the surface with a spectacular
display of aggression, white water and feathers. Feathers?
A never-ending stream of feathers appeared from the
pike's jaws. They looked completely out of place and
floated slowly away in all directions as the pike kicked and
thrashed. I had been right about a coot diving in the spot

all along, only it went down to the bottom in the pike's gullet and shortly afterwards that same pike had the audacity to grab my plug.

Considering these stories, it is difficult to believe that there are times when pike can turn extremely sensitive, refusing baits or lures which they sense to be 'attached' to something. However, on well-fished waters where the pike receive regular attention, their natural caution alerts them to danger, and they reject food which is repeatedly presented in the same way. They also learn to refuse the same baits placed in the same spots. They are no different in this from the canal roach that ends up in the matchman's keep-net every few weeks having sucked up a single caster, but which in between is infinitely easier to catch on a different bait and using a different method of presentation.

Those odd occurrences when we catch a pike and return it, only to have the very same pike grab hold again an hour later, tend to make us believe that because it has teeth and is a predator, the pike is less sensitive than non-predators. Don't believe it. Pike are better equipped physically – in the hunting senses of sight, hearing and sonar – than all the fish they catch and eat, which includes every species of fish that swims in freshwater. Otherwise their prey would get away and the pike would starve.

The pike's wonderful coloration and its camouflage pattern, both of which change to blend in with its surroundings, are unequalled among freshwater species. In clear water the prominent grey-green colour, the zigzag markings across its back and the intricate pattern of blotches or spots along its flanks are accentuated, and help to camouflage it as it lies in wait between reed stalks or tree stumps. However, in heavily coloured water the pike changes colour accordingly. When rivers are in full flood and the colour of milky tea, or when the water of a broad, pit or lake turns peaty or brownish due to strong winds disturbing the bottom sediment, the pike takes on a low-key colour scheme. The intensity of the spots against the usually contrasting background colour of its flanks is greatly reduced, and the beige, brown and yellow in its body coloration are emphasized, so that its form blends into the bottom silt or decaying weed.

Pike tend to vary in colour from one clear water to another depending on the nature of the background, so it

Predator and prey. The pike's camouflage of irregular-shaped spots, blotches and zigzag bars blends perfectly into the sub-surface scene as it lies in wait for young roach.

would be impossible for even the most brilliant artist to provide an exact colour guide. This is why there is such a difference in colour among the pike photographed in this book. But as there could never be any possibility of the pike being mistaken for another species, as an inexperienced angler might confuse a roach with a rudd, for instance, it matters not. The long, sleek, torpedo-shaped body and flattened, pointed snout of the pike is better known even to non-fishermen than any other indigenous species.

Its ultimate weight potential in British waters is probably slightly better than 50 lb, although in most fisheries a 20-pounder is considered the specimen size to aim for. And in truth, pike of this calibre, which usually measure around 40 in, can turn up anywhere given a rich food source – from a gravel pit of little more than 1 acre to a narrow Lincolnshire drain you can almost jump across. That is the nice thing about the pike and pike fishing. It provides diverse, exciting sport with a fish that can be caught at any time from June through until March, almost regardless of weather conditions, and which can weigh anything from 2 to over 20 lb.

CHAPTER TWO

ABOUT PIKE

FEEDING

Pike catch their food by scavenging dead or dying fish from the bottom. They do this either by lying in wait between reed stems or the sub-surface woodwork of fallen trees or old stagings to ambush an unsuspecting fish, or by grouping together and herding a large shoal of fry and small fish into a small bay or boat dyke from which there is no escape other than running the gauntlet. Contrary to popular belief, pike also hunt their prey in open water by following shoals of roach, bream or perch.

A pike's open jaws, as would be seen by a small fish immediately before meeting its maker, are not the most welcoming sight. Embedded in the lower jaw is a series of large, piercing, crushing teeth with which the pike both grips and immobilizes its prey; set into the roof of its mouth are hundreds of much smaller teeth all pointing backwards towards the throat, so there is only one

By simulating small fish, which often disappear from sight in one quick flash of the jaws, artificial lures irritate the pike into making a lunge.

direction for its food to go. Only a small percentage of the fish gripped between these powerful jaws ever get away. Occasionally one catches a small roach or bream that was lucky, and still has the scars to prove it, but not often.

Small fish often disappear in one quick flash of the jaws and are gulped down immediately. Larger meals, on the other hand, are gripped sideways tightly between the jaws until almost dead, then turned with the help of the tongue (sandpapery to the touch) and swallowed head first.

As with all freshwater species, the pike's metabolic rate is greatly retarded in low temperatures, so in the most severe of winter weather it eats far less than during the summer months and is much slower about it. The implications of this for the fisherman are that in warm water the pike gulps its food down quickly, and in cold water it takes its time about turning and swallowing the same-sized meal.

This is a point well worth remembering if you are presenting large baits and are continually experiencing missed fish on the strike. In all probability, the bait will not have been turned by the pike when you attempt to put the hooks home. The pike feels undue pressure from the rod tip, and promptly opens its mouth and ejects the bait. This chain of events can sometimes actually be seen through clear water, even at the end of the fight just before you net the fish, when the head and tail of the bait are clearly visible either side of the pike's jaws. The fact is that at no time during the fight did the pike release its grip on the bait with a view to turning it so that the hooks could catch hold. And of course at this late stage the pike swims off with a disgruntled look on its face and minus its meal, which it releases at the last moment.

The pike possesses exceptional eyesight, which enables it to capture its prey and evade enemies. In addition, it can determine the presence of other fish and other objects, even when it cannot see them, by way of a highly sensitive nervous system. This operates through tiny ducts connected by cords to the lateral line, which runs the entire length of the pike's body from gill plate to tail root. These ducts or sense organs detect vibrations, sound and even sudden pressure changes. On the head there are additional sensors, in the form of small holes around the eyes and beneath the chin running along the undersides of the lower jaw.

Esox has a highly developed sense of smell, too. When its other senses are effectively reduced through the lack of movement of its prey, or by poor visibility (in heavily coloured water, for instance), the aroma of a dead fish lying static on the bottom enables the pike to locate it easily, especially in flowing water when the pike simply follows the scent trail up to the food source.

So acute are these senses that even totally blind pike are able to lunge confidently at a live fish or an artificial lure, or sniff up a dead fish from the bottom (see 'Fishing at night' p. 101).

In addition to consuming other fish including its own kind, plus rodents and water birds, the pike eats amphibians such as newts, frogs and toads and larger crustaceans like the crayfish. It will, if given the chance and in a hungry mood, have a go at virtually anything edible. I can well remember an incident that happened many years back that illustrates this point perfectly. At the time I was ledgering with two rods for tench in a beautiful estate lake. It was high summer, and around mid morning I decided to call it a day, not having had the slightest interest shown in my two baits. On one rod was a freelined whole mussel, and on the other ledgered sausage-meat paste. I had in fact scattered a dozen or so large lumps of paste around the area close to the bait, just on the fringe of some overhanging willows – usually a productive spot.

I wound in the paste rod, and had started retrieving the mussel when all of a sudden up from the bottom came a long, thin pike of about 7 lb which promptly grabbed the mussel on the surface. Fortunately the hook ended up in the scissors away from the teeth and I landed the pike. But there, welling up in its throat, was a huge lump of sausage paste. The pike must have sucked up all the loose pieces before it hit the mussel. No doubt eventually it would have sucked up the hook paste, too.

Pike are also partial to twitched lobworms and I wish I had a fiver for each one caught or lost when twitching worms and slugs for chub. Even bread flake attracts them; but then something white and fluffy bouncing about in the current is guaranteed to produce a reaction, whether through irritation, aggression, territorial pride or hunger.

As with all species, pike relate their feeding to light values. On some days, when pike are coming out thick and

*When the light values
suddenly increase on
overcast days, the pike
in deep-coloured lakes
or pits often respond
immediately.*

fast to whatever is offered them, this would not appear to
be so. But on other occasions, particularly during the
winter months when the sky may be heavily overcast all
day, it might need the sun's rays to break through the
clouds for only an hour to trigger off a feeding spree. I
have noticed this on so many occasions, and most
particularly when presenting static deadbaits on the bottom
of deep, heavily coloured pits and lakes. Fish which have
been lying dormant for several hours are suddenly motiv-
ated into moving by the increased light values. And when
pike are moving, they are willing to feed. So while
sunlight penetrates the gloom, runs on static deadbaits can
be expected, but when it disappears again the pike seem to
lose interest.

   Is it that the shoals of small fish start to feed and move
about when the light increases by several stops that attracts
pike? Or is it simply that in water with increased visibility

brought about by a sudden burst of sunlight, pike know that hunting their prey will be easier. Either way, it is the sudden and drastic change in light values which triggers their natural hunting and feeding instincts.

REPRODUCTION

Pike spawn earlier than most other coarse fish species: usually during the month of April (possibly in the latter part of March following a mild winter). I am not totally against the theory that Mother Nature has organized it this way purposefully, because old *Esox* is then ready for the inevitable banquet which occurs several weeks later when shoal fish like roach, rudd and bream gather by the thousands on the shallows for spawning, presenting week upon week of easy meals.

Because of the rich, extra food source, gravel pit and reservoir trout fisheries produce the largest pike within the British Isles. Spawn-laden females like this near 40-pounder, taken by Dan Leary from a Norfolk trout water, contains up to 6–7 lb of eggs.

Accompanied by up to three or four eager and much smaller males, often referred to as 'jacks' (male pike are thought rarely to attain much heavier weights than 12–13 lb), the female, heavy with spawn, seeks out shallow weedy areas where the eggs can be shed. When soft weeds are absent any fibrous medium is used, such as the foliage of sunken bushes or trees, sedges, reed or rush stems. Pike have even been known to move on to flooded meadows or marshlands, laying the spawn among the long grass.

The commotion made by pike spawning in the shallows can be heard from a long way off on a still day. With jacks in attendance ready to spray milt over the eggs as she sheds them, the shuddering noise made by a large female in the act is quite distinct. A non-angler wandering along close by could easily believe that a couple of dogs were chasing each other through the water, the disturbance is that loud.

The eggs hatch within two weeks and the fry, which keep close to the weeds for safety, grow rapidly; initially they feed on a diet of plankton and minute crustacea, followed by aquatic insects and, at a very early age, the fry of other fish including their own kind. Really weedy lakes, full of Canadian pondweed, for instance, inevitably contain an unusually prolific head of small pike because the survival rate of the fry protected by dense vegetation is greater than in less weedy environments.

The proportion of eggs to bodyweight carried by a healthy female is quite considerable. A 20-pounder, for instance, might be carrying up to 3 or 4 lb, and the spawn in a 40-pounder could weigh as much as 6–7 lb. The monstrous 35–45 lb pike taken from trout fisheries in recent years have truly enormous roes. And with a rich diet of trout to gorge on, plus coarse species of all weights and size ranges from fry upwards, no wonder more huge pike are taken from trout reservoirs than anywhere else within the British Isles. Even the huge Irish and Scottish lochs that have produced so many of the biggest pike in years gone by now have to take second place behind the trout reservoirs. The most famous reservoir for producing these jumbo pike is of course Llandegfedd in Wales. When this 450 acre trout fishery was opened for just a fortnight's trial run in October 1989 no less than four pike over 40 lb. were caught.

DISTRIBUTION

Within the British Isles no other fish enjoys such wide distribution as the pike. Indeed, there cannot be many fisheries in either still or running water in which the pike does not help maintain the delicate balance between predator and prey. Only modern, man-made fisheries and carp-only waters, where the balancing presence of the pike is not required because only mature fish are introduced, are not purposefully stocked with pike. On a world-wide basis, the pike is exceptionally well represented. It is fished for across the entire northern hemisphere from North America and Canada all the way across Europe and even into Northern Asia.

CHAPTER THREE

LOCATING PIKE

Just like their prey river pike are attracted to features, a fact which this young angler is obviously well aware of.

A S pike do not shoal as such, although they do group together at various times, location is not quite the same as with other species. You need to find the pike's preferred habitat rather than individual fish. For instance, with tench you look for their bubbles, which tell you exactly where they are. Bream can be seen rolling on the surface and they too send up bubbles, so their position can be pinpointed by looking through binoculars. Carp also bubble, so you know exactly where they are – even the position of an individual fish feeding on the bottom of

heavily coloured water. And when carp take floaters from the surface, even their size can be assessed.

With many species, observation alone will tell you their exact position immediately, but this is not usually the case with pike. The odd occasion does present itself when pike can be seen through clear water and offered a bait, and it is then fun, and most enlightening, to watch their subsequent reactions. Generally speaking, however, and this applies to most methods of pike fishing, you need to select likely areas. You do this using a combination of imagination, watercraft, perseverance and a knowledge of the various ambush habitats preferred by pike, taking into account water and weather conditions, and the availability of prey fish. It is not as complicated as it sounds.

RIVERS

Consider the features of a typical, medium-paced river, for instance (see fig. 1). As pike never wish to be far from their next meal, they tend to occupy the obvious habitats where

FIGURE 1 *River habitats: features where pike lie in ambush*

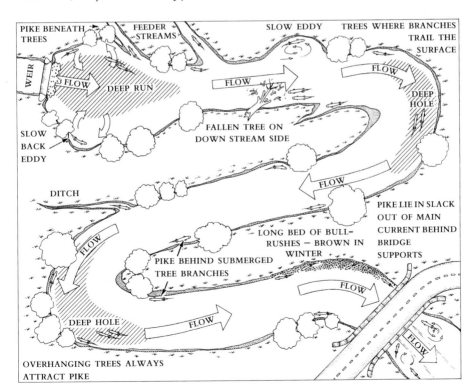

PIKE BENEATH TREES   FEEDER STREAMS   SLOW EDDY   TREES WHERE BRANCHES TRAIL THE SURFACE

WEIR   FLOW   DEEP RUN   FLOW   FLOW   DEEP HOLE

SLOW BACK EDDY   FALLEN TREE ON DOWN STREAM SIDE

DITCH   FLOW

PIKE LIE IN SLACK OUT OF MAIN CURRENT BEHIND BRIDGE SUPPORTS

FLOW   LONG BED OF BULL-RUSHES — BROWN IN WINTER

PIKE BEHIND SUBMERGED TREE BRANCHES   FLOW

DEEP HOLE   FLOW   FLOW

OVERHANGING TREES ALWAYS ATTRACT PIKE

shoals of dace, roach, bream or chub live. In short: find its prey and you will have found the pike.

Take my local River Wensum, for example. All the best roach or chub swims in the upper, non-tidal reaches also happen to contain at least one big, double-figure pike plus the inevitable collection of jacks or lesser fish. And this is no coincidence. Looked at in reverse, if I happen to latch on to a big pike while out lure fishing a previously unfished stretch, I will mentally mark the area down for future exploration when after roach or chub.

Only very rarely are pike found fighting the current in really fast, turbulent swims; the effort required expends too much energy. Besides, they are lazy and much prefer to lie in wait to ambush shoal fish as they pass by. So expect to find pike behind clumps of bullrushes, tall reeds, sunken trees, in slow back-eddies, deep channels, sudden depressions in the riverbed, in holes on the bends, at the confluence of a ditch or side stream and the main river, in weir and mill pools and so on. During the summer months pike love to lie in wait among the huge lettuce-type leaves (usually called cabbages) of the yellow water-lily which fringes the margins of slow-moving rivers and their backwaters (see 'Lure fishing' p. 111). Once the frosts of winter destroy the lily-beds, pike seek the sanctuary of deeper areas and alternative ambush points.

For much of the time, both summer and winter, the pike lives in close proximity to its prey, often lying mere feet away from, say, a shoal of roach. These tolerate its presence, knowing full well that until it is aroused they have little to fear. However, they soon become agitated and very alert when they sense a predator moving in for the kill, and they close ranks in mock security when the pike sets its fins and starts slowly to curl its tail in gentle waves – the classic pose from which it makes those sudden, explosive lunges.

Knowledge of the various depths in each swim along a river's course is the greatest short cut to catching pike and catching them quickly. If you fish the river regularly for other species, you will no doubt already have such details logged in your mind in readiness for pike fishing during the winter, when the water is substantially more coloured and the bottom contours cannot be seen.

If you know the depth of a swim, you can trot a livebait

downstream at the most productive depth, which is from 1 to 2 ft off bottom (just above the pike), or retrieve a wobbled deadbait or an artificial lure immediately above the bottom contours in that same layer without snagging upon every other cast and continually having to pull for a break in the line. The latter is not exactly conducive to putting pike on the bank. And to leave multi-hook rigs or lures on the bottom is not only costly, it is extremely harmful to wildlife.

Try to visualize in your mind's eye how the pike will be lying in low water temperatures, with its lower fins almost touching bottom. Winter pike invariably carry numerous parasites like double-sucker leeches, which cling to their fins, proving their preference for the bottom strata of mud and silt. Obviously a moving bait needs to be presented in that 2 ft layer of water immediately above the bottom – a point that should always be considered.

In mild weather, pike will willingly leave the bottom and rush several feet upwards to intercept a bait near the surface, creating a glorious vicious swirl in the process. During the summer you can expect them to move double the distance because in warm water, when their metabolic rate is working overtime, pike are unbelievably aggressive and always willing to have a go. This, of course, applies to all waters, not just rivers. It is true they are noticeably thinner and weigh less in summer, but they certainly make up for it by fighting like demons, and repeatedly tail-walk when held hard. In fact, I do not understand why most anglers think of the pike as a winter-only species. Sport during the warmer months can be wonderfully hectic, particularly with surface lures (see 'Summer plugging' p. 116). But in the cold depths of winter when increased water colour reduces visibility, your bait needs to be placed close by the fish, and sometimes right on their noses, or you won't catch many pike.

STILLWATERS

In most stillwaters the deep-water habitats into which small shoal fish like perch, roach, bream and rudd move to spend the winter months, once vegetation cover has

Deep weir pools such as the Denver Sluice shown here, which empties waters of the Great Ouse system into the Relief Channel, attract enormous concentrations of shoal fish and thus become prime winter pike hot spots.

disappeared, and thus where pike may also be found, are not always obvious.

Indeed, compared to river systems, which are easy to read because most pike habitats stand out clearly, stillwaters require much preparatory work with a plummet to obtain an accurate plan of the bottom contours. After all, one sheet of water looks more or less like another once leaves have left the trees, the marginal rushes have died back, and the surface plants have rotted away. Compared to summer, the stillwater in winter takes on unfriendly proportions, which are exaggerated by cold weather, heavy rain, strong winds, or a mixture of these. But have faith; the fish have not jumped out onto dry land. They are all still there, they just have to be located.

If a boat is available plummeting is much easier, especially on large fisheries, but by far the quickest results

Systematic plummeting of a gravel pit to pinpoint the deeper holes and gullies where shoal fish congregate during the colder months produced this lovely brace for illustrator and fellow angling writer, Dave Batten

are achieved by using an echo-sounder such as one of the portable Humminbird fish-finders, which not only provide a digital depth read-out, but actually indicate both shoals and even individual fish situated beneath the boat on the display screen (see 'Tackle' p. 58).

However, only a small percentage of pike anglers at the moment use, or indeed can even afford, such modern technology. So let us assume that a plan of the bottom contours will be arrived at by old-fashioned means – the good old plummet used in conjunction with a sliding float that can be moved up and down the line to gauge the exact depth. For this job, a 2 oz bomb tied direct to the reel line is perfect for easy casting, and where long distances are necessary. Tie on a nylon sliding stop knot above the sliding float and you have the perfect plummeting rig.

If it helps, take along a clipboard and foolscap paper, and

as you plumb each section fill in the respective depths on an outline of the fishery. It is not only fun and workmanlike; the results will stand you in good stead for many years to come. The pike fisherman who cannot tell you the approximate depth of the water into which his bait has been cast does not deserve to catch much – and invariably doesn't.

Stillwaters come in all shapes and sizes, from 500 acre broads and reservoirs down to pits and lakes of little more than an acre or two, and to illustrate every type and permutation of bottom structure would take a whole book in itself. However, because gravel pits contain most of the features found in other kinds of stillwaters, and have on average more variations per 100 yd than any other, they provide an interesting challenge and a valuable learning ground. Although a huge pit can look most formidable to the newcomer, especially in bad weather when white-water waves build up and crash against the shoreline, beneath the surface it has a very special character, made up of deeps and shallows particular only to that sheet of

FIGURE 2 *Still-waters: locating pike within a large gravel pit complex*

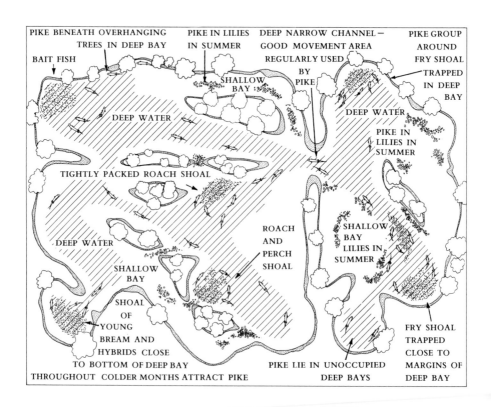

PIKE BENEATH OVERHANGING TREES IN DEEP BAY

PIKE IN LILIES IN SUMMER

DEEP NARROW CHANNEL – GOOD MOVEMENT AREA REGULARLY USED BY PIKE

PIKE GROUP AROUND FRY SHOAL TRAPPED IN DEEP BAY

BAIT FISH

SHALLOW BAY

DEEP WATER

DEEP WATER

PIKE IN LILIES IN SUMMER

TIGHTLY PACKED ROACH SHOAL

DEEP WATER

ROACH AND PERCH SHOAL

SHALLOW BAY LILIES IN SUMMER

SHALLOW BAY

SHOAL OF YOUNG BREAM AND HYBRIDS CLOSE TO BOTTOM OF DEEP BAY THROUGHOUT COLDER MONTHS ATTRACT PIKE

PIKE LIE IN UNOCCUPIED DEEP BAYS

FRY SHOAL TRAPPED CLOSE TO MARGINS OF DEEP BAY

water. And these you must discover and be able to pinpoint in order to catch pike.

Consider, for instance, the multitude of features in fig. 2, which is part of a typical gravel pit complex. The minerals have been removed in a series of clearly defined channels creating a network of deep gullies, holes and bays separated by tree-clad islands and shallow bars or plateaux. Old gravel workings such as this, excavated during World War 2 for the purpose of building roads and airfields, have matured into beautiful environments completely over-grown along the margins, with thick beds of reeds fringing the shallows, and features like overhanging trees providing additional winter pike habitats wherever they shade the surface of deep water close in.

Small shoal fish always seek the sanctuary of deep water during low water temperatures, a fact of which pike are only too aware, so most of the shallow areas of this particular pit can be discounted. It is true that, whatever the conditions, a small proportion of the pit's pike population will be scattered around the margins, even in ridiculously shallow water beside reed-beds, old lily roots and the like. However, the bulk of the pike, especially the larger fish, spend most of their time working the gullies, holes or deep bays feeding from the heavy concentrations of small shoal fish that congregate there. During the autumn, before the water temperature drops drastically and before really chilly weather sets in, these same shoals of small fish will become more widely spread, roaming along the edges of drop-offs into deep water and in mid-depth plateaux or bays. The exact position of these shoals, and so to some extent the pike, is determined by the clouds of zooplankton upon which the small fish feed. So if, for instance, the wind blows hard in a particular direction for a couple of days and the sub-surface tow pushes mountains of zooplankton into a particular bay, the shoal fish will follow. And they in turn will be followed by the pike, which tend to pack or group around the perimeter of the shoal, lunging in for a meal when the fancy takes them.

The visible sign of this activity is dozens of fry scattering repeatedly on the surface as pike strike from beneath. But you need to make hay while the sun shines, because when the wind changes and moves the food of the shoal fish, they and the pike will also move.

Providing the perfect ambush point from which to surprise passing shoal fish, thick reed beds are used by pike to good effect. Small bays and inlets are guaranteed hot spots.

As I have already mentioned, there will always be pike scattered along the margins in and around reed-beds. And of course in shallow stillwaters that are nowhere deeper than about 4 ft – such as lakes, meres and broads – thick reed-beds are the only habitats left once winter frosts have removed lilies and soft weeds. So you have a good idea of where the pike will be lying. What is more, if the water remains clear, as it is likely to if the weather stays cold, still and frosty, the shoals of fish upon which the pike preys will also seek sanctuary in the reeds, thus creating fabulous hotspots wherever the water is deep enough. However, not all thick reed-beds will contain pike, although viewed from a boat or the bank the potential would look to be the same all the way around the perimeter.

Depth is the critical factor in these shallow stillwaters. Consider fig. 3, for instance, a shallow Norfolk Broad, although it could be a mere, a lake or even an Irish lough or a shallow gravel or sand pit. Along one shoreline the reeds are sparse and covered by only a few inches of water, a fact which is not always obvious in the dim light of dawn, or when fishing from a distance. But along the opposite shoreline not only is the reed-line thicker, it extends further back into the marshland. This potentially gives

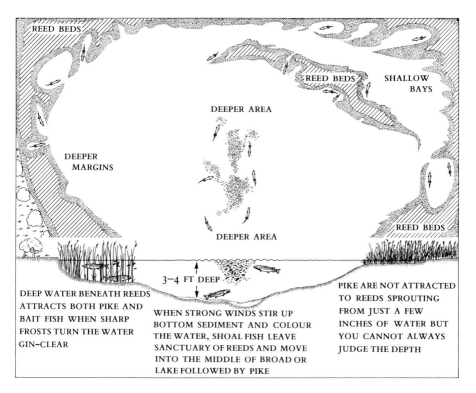

REED BEDS

REED BEDS SHALLOW BAYS

DEEPER AREA

DEEPER MARGINS

REED BEDS

DEEPER AREA

3-4 FT DEEP

DEEP WATER BENEATH REEDS ATTRACTS BOTH PIKE AND BAIT FISH WHEN SHARP FROSTS TURN THE WATER GIN-CLEAR

WHEN STRONG WINDS STIR UP BOTTOM SEDIMENT AND COLOUR THE WATER, SHOAL FISH LEAVE SANCTUARY OF REEDS AND MOVE INTO THE MIDDLE OF BROAD OR LAKE FOLLOWED BY PIKE

PIKE ARE NOT ATTRACTED TO REEDS SPROUTING FROM JUST A FEW INCHES OF WATER BUT YOU CANNOT ALWAYS JUDGE THE DEPTH

more space for both pike and compacted shoals of small fish, among reeds which have their roots in a good 3 ft of water.

In really rough weather pike leave the reeds because they dislike the constant movement of stems knocking against their bodies. I suspect this interferes with their complicated sensory system (see 'About Pike' p. 16). But then, as the water becomes coloured through the disturbance of the bottom sediment when the wind rips across shallow open water, the shoal fish are given the confidence they need to vacate the reeds and feed amongst the particles within the suspension. And the pike follow them. Pike are then ready to accept a bait presented in just about any spot in the broad.

The occasional flip on the surface of a small shoal fish, or grebes or cormorants continually working the same small area (and don't forget the binoculars), or even the scattering of fry, all point to the biggest concentrations of shoal fish in coloured water, and the pike won't be far away.

FIGURE 3 *A typical broad: in shallow still-waters no deeper than 3 to 4 ft, reed-beds provide the only habitat for both pike and their prey*

CHAPTER FOUR

TACKLE

THE pike tackle of yesteryear was exceptionally crude. No one paid much attention to the enjoyment to be had from the fight, but were only concerned with putting fish on the bank. Nowadays, thanks to the lightness yet unbelievable strength of carbon fibre, we can select a particular outfit for the job at hand or a general combo capable of dealing with most situations in pike fishing. It depends on how specialized you want to become.

RODS

Test curves

When it comes to selecting a pike rod from the tackle dealer's shelves, look immediately above the handle where the test curve rating is usually written. Most specialist two-piece rods of 11 or 12 ft are rated in order to provide you with an idea of the rod's power. You multiply the respective test curve by 5 to arrive at the suggested line strength for that rod so that both rod and line will stretch simultaneously instead of one before the other – the main reason for those instant snap-offs on the rod or line. A rod with a test curve of, say, 2¼ lb means that its suggested line strength is around 11 lb. To arrive at the lower limit of lines that can safely be used, multiply by 4 (which in this case gives 9 lb), and then by 6 for the upper limit (13½ lb). So a 2¼ lb test curve rod will comfortably handle lines between 9 and 13½ lb. The perfect all-round, general-purpose pike rod is probably one around 2–2½ lb test curve. Go much lighter and you risk casting heavy baits on too light a line. Go heavier and you won't enjoy the fight given by most of the pike you catch. A heavier line is only needed for distance casting.

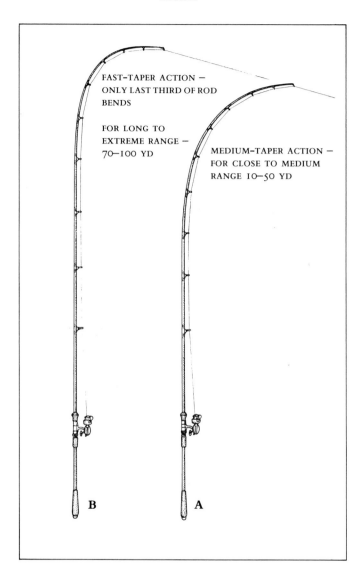

FIGURE 4 *Pike rod actions*

FAST-TAPER ACTION –
ONLY LAST THIRD OF ROD
BENDS

FOR LONG TO
EXTREME RANGE –
70–100 YD

MEDIUM-TAPER ACTION –
FOR CLOSE TO MEDIUM
RANGE 10–50 YD

B   A

Action

Two distinct types of action should be considered when choosing a pike rod (regardless of test curve) based on whether the vast majority of your fishing will be at close to medium range (10–60 yd) or long to extreme range (70–100 yd). For the former a medium tip action (fig. 4) which is fairly snappy for casting but eventually develops

For all close to medium-range piking, whether fishing from a boat or bank, a medium-tip action rod of 2–2¼ lb test curve is sufficient to subdue the lunges of big fish while allowing you to enjoy the fight from pike of all sizes.

into a progressive curve when under full pressure, is perfect. It helps to absorb the lunges of a powerful pike while retaining a degree of stability for picking up line and setting the hooks.

For long to extreme range work a considerably meatier, fast-taper action is required. It should possess sufficient backbone for punching deadbaits out a long way and for picking maximum line up on the strike, whether ledgering or presenting the bait beneath a drift float rig.

Something to remember with powerful long-range rods, some of which have a test curve of 3 lb, is that you cannot expect such a tool to bend nicely into a full curve when a big fish thumps away directly beneath the rod tip and to remain rigid for casting and striking. So extra care must be taken as a pike that has been hooked at long range is played progressively closer to the bank.

Although there are a few carbon/glass composite rods at the cheaper end of the price range, the lightest and most reliable blanks are made from a high percentage of carbon, which of course is also more enjoyable to use. Specialist carbon pike rods manufactured by Ryobi, Tri Cast, Daiwa and North Western are particularly recommended.

It is perhaps worth mentioning at this stage that any carp rod with similar test curves and action to those described will serve admirably for catching pike and vice versa. After all, they are fish within the same size range, the only difference being that pike have teeth. So there is no need to buy duplicate outfits. In fact, many manufacturers use exactly the same carbon blanks for pike rods as those sold for carp, although customizing and decoration tend to hide this.

Length

For most of my fishing, covering a variety of waters both large and small, and for most livebaiting and deadbaiting, I prefer the versatility of a two-piece 12-footer. For close range work, especially where the banks are overhung by

For close-range fishing where the banks are heavily overgrown 11 ft rods are most practical. But when presenting baits into large, deep rivers and lakes, 12 ft models are more versatile and provide maximum line pick up.

trees, 11 ft models would naturally prove more practical. And this is how you should view the situation, remembering of course that longer rods pick up more line and are more efficient for controlling fish around margins that are heavily overgrown with tall reeds, sunken trees and the like. I even prefer longer rods when pike fishing sitting in a boat, because casting is so much easier. In addition, the extra length allows a big fish to be held well away from the anchor ropes.

My complaint about most commercially made pike rods, most rods for that matter (you can always make your own from blanks), is that the handle unit is placed far too high, resulting in up to a foot of useless rod sticking out behind my elbow and getting in the way when playing fish; plus the fact that it is also a complete waste of money. Ideally you need no more than a good allowance for the hand grip (for casting), plus the length of the forearm. The reel seat should then be situated immediately beneath your hand. I can see no reason whatsoever (except that some people consider long handles look trendy) why the distance between butt cap and reel stem should be any more than 22–24 in at the outside. My own rods have even shorter handles.

Lure rods

While an 11 ft rod can be used for lure fishing at a pinch, with continual casting it becomes extremely tiring to use after a while. The tiredness factor, together with the fact that the snappier action of a lure rod allows the artificial to be worked more attractively, makes an 8½ or 9 ft rod more pleasurable to use. Again, there is little reason for more than a comfortable length between reel stem and butt cap, so reject any rod which protrudes beyond the elbow.

Some manufacturers provide a choice of handle grips suited to both fixed-spool and multiplying reels. However, in the case of handles for multipliers, the stability given to the multiplier rod by a trigger grip built into the reel fitting makes for far more comfortable casting and retrieving than those without.

Though they are considered a highly specialized part of the rod manufacturing industry, a limited market leading to lack of choice (only ABU currently produce suitable models), the 5–6 ft single-handed, trigger-grip American bait-casting rods offer the chance of extra fun with pike on artificials. Being stiff, these wand-like sticks are far better for imparting live action to artificials, especially surface-popping plugs and buzz baits, compared to the longer, traditional spinning rods, which tend to absorb much of your arm movement instead of transferring it directly to the plug. Coupled to a baby, magnetic, cast-control multiplier there is no finer outfit for working artificials at close range and into awkward places.

REELS

Without question, a medium to large format (not giant) fixed-spool reel is the best overall choice for pike fishing, capable of handling any eventuality. My advice would be to invest in a good-quality, ball-bearing model with two spools so that you always have a spare fitted with fresh line. It should have the capacity to hold around 200 yd of 10–12 lb test; and a strong bale arm assembly incorporating a roller so that the minimum amount of friction is created when a pike rips line from the spool. This, of course, only really applies if, like me, you play pike on the slipping clutch and not by backwinding, which seems to be in vogue with many young fishermen nowadays.

I would suggest, however, that using the slipping clutch for the purpose for which it was invented, so that the spool rotates and gives line before reaching full load, is the most effective way of ensuring that a pike takes no more line than you need to give. This becomes more important when you are trying to control a lively fish in limited space between snags.

It takes but a second to tighten the drag knob until line may be pulled firmly yet smoothly from the spool (not so loose that the spool turns when retrieving the bait, because then line twist will develop). Practice soon makes perfect, and you will learn to play even a large fish with complete confidence knowing it can take line at any time during the fight without the slightest chance of a break-off.

We now come to choosing the best type of drag: a reel

*For maximum fun
with pike of any size,
and for imparting live
action to lures, there is
nothing more effective
than the American
short, stiff, trigger-
grip handle, bait-
casting rods.*

with a standard front-adjusting clutch (built into the spool itself), as in the famous Mitchell 300 series, or the now very popular skirted-spool, rear- or stern-drag reel upon which most new models are based.

Old-fashioned, front-drag reels are less complicated and put less torque on the system because only the spool rotates, not the entire rotor assembly as with rear drags, which creates potentially more wear. Most anglers, however, seem to find clutch adjustment easier with rear-drag reels, and line does not accidentally slip down between spool and rotor-housing as it can on front drags. So there it is. There are pros and cons with both types, and at the end of the day it is a matter of personal preference, because if you feel happy using a particular reel you will undoubtedly catch more fish with it.

In recent years, reels fitted with long-nosed, tapered or 'coned' spools have become extremely popular among pike anglers wishing to add extra yards to their casting range, and the super-smooth models by Shimano, Ryobi and Daiwa are particularly recommended for very long range work.

A facility fitted to several makes of reels whereby the spool can be disengaged from the gearing so that it rotates and gives line to a biting fish, much used by carp anglers in conjunction with the bolt rig and closed bale arm, works far less efficiently with pike. Well-educated pike, wary of the slightest resistance when sucking up a static deadbait from the bottom, will quickly reject it even with the free spool facility set at its lightest tension.

For catching pike, high gear ratios creating a super-fast retrieve are nowhere near so important as manufacturers would have us believe. In fact, techniques of wobbling deadbaits, plugging, spinning, and so on, are made more difficult by a fast-retrieve reel. Also, playing fish is more pleasurable with reels of standard gear ratios. So beware of merchandizing promises. A wide, long spool, so the line comes off in large loose coils, is far more important for smooth, long casts and exact bait presentation.

Multipliers

When coupled to short trigger-handled rods (although all types of reel fittings will accommodate multipliers) the baby, magnetic cast control multiplier provides accurate, trouble-free casting with the smallest lures, even tiny spinning jigs.

For presenting lures on both standard and short American-style, single-handed rods, and for piking on wild open waters such as reservoirs or the Irish and Scottish lochs, where fishing from boats into great depths at anchor, or trolling, puts greater demands on your tackle, the multiplying reel has much to offer. Indeed, the technique of trolling is almost impossible with a fixed-spool reel.

Top models nowadays are superbly engineered with lightweight duralium spools, friction-free level wind and magnetic cast control; all so necessary for trouble-free fishing. But these features naturally affect the price, and a multiplier which allows you to obtain the best results and maximum enjoyment from lure fishing costs at least twice the price of a good-quality, fixed-spool reel. I would even go so far as to say that unless you are prepared to invest in the right tool for the job do not buy one at all, because cheap multipliers will never allow you to enjoy lure fishing fully.

The Swedish manufacturers ABU lead the field with their range of Ambassador freshwater multipliers, closely followed by Daiwa and Ryobi. Even the tiniest models (a real delight to use when matched to a bait-casting stick) will accommodate 200 yd of 10–12 lb test, and for boat-work on large waters, when lines up to 18 lb may be needed for fishing over rocks or into heavy weeds, both the ABU 6000 series and Ryobi's T2 hold more than sufficient, up to 300 yd.

In recent years, lefthand-wind multipliers have become readily available. Some of the Ryobi models are ambidextrous, which allows you to hold the rod in your strongest hand while performing the simple task of winding in with the other, just like fixed-spool reels.

LINES

For the demands of pike fishing the ideal monofilament line should be abrasion-resistant, supple and possess a reasonable degree of stretch to absorb the pike's lunges and tail-walking antics. Under no circumstances should you use pre-stretched and thus 'thinner' mono lines, which fracture all too easily just when you need elasticity in the line to prevent the pike making off, possibly with a set of trebles deeply embedded in its throat.

Continual lure casting, or punching deadbaits out long distances, tests monofilament to its limit, so always use a slightly heavier breaking strain line than perhaps you really need to give yourself an extra safety margin. Most top brands can be purchased in bulk spools, which works out considerably cheaper than buying 100 yd at a time, and allows you to change over to fresh line regularly. There is nothing more irritating and irresponsible than losing and leaving the hooks in a big fish because you economized on such an inexpensive item as line.

For most pike fishing requirements Sylcast sorrel in 11 lb test is very reliable. Other brands such as Bayer Perlon and Maxima are also recommended.

For trolling, when setting the hooks with a long length of mono behind the boat proves troublesome, and for presenting baits at great distances beneath a sail-type drift float, low-stretch dacron is worth considering. There are brands that float and can be easily lifted from the surface to alleviate a bow when drifting in strong winds. At long range (100 yd plus) the fact that dacron has less stretch than standard monofilament increases the chances of the hooks penetrating the pike's bony jaws.

KNOTS

For tying monofilament to the swivel at the end of a spinning (a general term encompassing all lure fishing) trace, or to a snap tackle (see p. 46), or for tying line to any swivel used in the construction of pike rigs, I have complete faith in the 'mahseer knot' (fig. 5A). Its great strength lies in the fact that this knot stretches when under full strain, as opposed to some other knots, which constrict and thus prematurely fracture long before the line has been pulled beyond its degree of elasticity.

To construct a stop knot on the line above a sliding float, the five-turn stop knot shown in fig. 5B is perfect. It can be made from several inches of the reel line, or from 10–20 lb power gum, which stays in position and creates minimal friction. Remember *not* to trim the ends off short. Leave

FIGURE 5 *Knots*

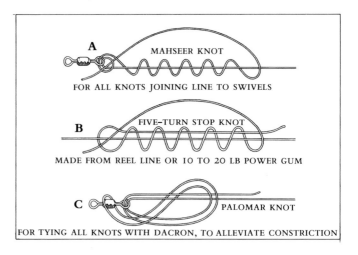

them 1–1½ in long so they fold when the line passes backwards and forwards through the rings without catching and causing a sudden halt, which if it occurs at the wrong moment might just cost you a lost fish.

For tying dacron to the eye of a swivel, the best knot to use is the Palomar (fig. 5C) because it does not constrict under any kind of pressure. Do not use blood knots, tucked or otherwise, because a premature fracture could arise.

HOOKS TRACES AND SWIVELS

Hooks

There is a very large range of different types of treble hooks for making livebait and deadbait traces and for replacing the rusted or broken hooks on artificial lures.

From the start I must say that while I prefer to fish lures with barbs on the hooks, for all live- and deadbait pike fishing I use only semi-barbless trebles. Semi-barbless means that one barb is left on one prong only of the treble, for holding on the bait, leaving the two barbless hooks for hooking. Reliable makes include the Partridge outbends, the Drennan carbon semi-barbless, and the Eagle Claw in-turn point (which needs to be doctored by flattening two of the barbs with pliers or forceps before use). Hook

Even when situated well down, semi-barbless hooks are easily removed with long-nosed artery forceps without harm to pike or the fisherman.

removal is much easier with semi-barbless hooks, especially if you are presenting static deadbaits, when the occasional deeply hooked pike is inevitable.

For really heavy work, Partridge make a super-strong treble hook which, though rather thick in the wire, can safely be used even on lines up to 20 lb test for the occasional situations that demand extra-heavy gear.

Trace wire

Trace wire is available in two types: cabled alasticum, which is easily workable, and can be twisted by hand around the eye of the treble or swivel (see fig. 6) and the slightly more springy, yet finer-diameter wire, such as Drennan bronze-tinted Seven Strand, or Marlin Steel which is available in green or brown. Both require crimping with narrow-gauge ferrules (such as Drennan 'slim crimps') for a neat, strong join.

Cabled alasticum in 15 lb test (it is available at 10–15, 20 and 25 lb) provides sufficient strength for both spinning traces and two-hook traces, more commonly called 'snap tackles'. Because springy brands are slightly narrower in diameter than cabled alasticum, for most pike fishing you can afford to step up to 20 lb test to provide a safety margin.

In very clear water, when offering the bait to educated pike which have been fished regularly, a reduction to 15 lb or even 10 lb wire can induce more pick-ups because it allows the bait to behave more naturally.

Trace-making

To make a simple 10 in spinning trace with cabled alasticum (longer traces have the habit of kinking prematurely and are not necessary for working lures), pass the end through one eye of the swivel and through again, making sure that the end comes out through the coil (see fig. 6A). After pulling tight, firmly wind the end of the wire around itself as in fig. 6B, using thumb and forefinger. A 1-in long end is quite sufficient with

FIGURE 6 *Making traces*

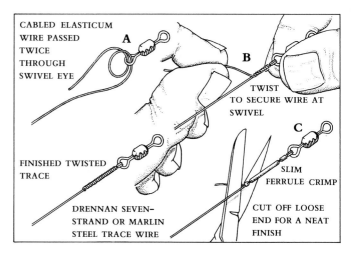

CABLED ELASTICUM WIRE PASSED TWICE THROUGH SWIVEL EYE

A

B

TWIST TO SECURE WIRE AT SWIVEL

FINISHED TWISTED TRACE

C

SLIM FERRULE CRIMP

DRENNAN SEVEN-STRAND OR MARLIN STEEL TRACE WIRE

CUT OFF LOOSE END FOR A NEAT FINISH

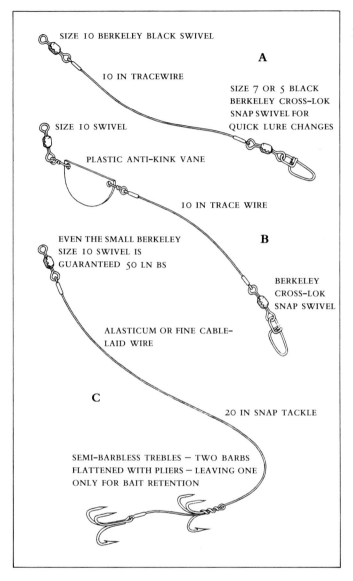

SIZE 10 BERKELEY BLACK SWIVEL

A

10 IN TRACEWIRE

SIZE 7 OR 5 BLACK
BERKELEY CROSS-LOK
SNAP SWIVEL FOR
SIZE 10 SWIVEL   QUICK LURE CHANGES

PLASTIC ANTI-KINK VANE

10 IN TRACE WIRE

EVEN THE SMALL BERKELEY   **B**
SIZE 10 SWIVEL IS
GUARANTEED 50 LN BS

BERKELEY
CROSS-LOK
SNAP SWIVEL

ALASTICUM OR FINE CABLE-
LAID WIRE

C

20 IN SNAP TACKLE

SEMI-BARBLESS TREBLES — TWO BARBS
FLATTENED WITH PLIERS — LEAVING ONE
ONLY FOR BAIT RETENTION

FIGURE 7 *Traces*

alasticum because its strength lies in the fact that the wire
has been passed twice around the swivel eye and trapped.
To ensure that the prickly end of the cabled wire does not
catch on the reel line, firmly give a few quick turns with
thumb and forefinger in the direction in which it was
wound, to bed it in.

When trace-making with the finer, springy wire and
slim crimps, follow exactly the initial procedure in fig. 6
for the holding knot, then sleeve on a slim crimp and

Tail-walking pike put maximum strain on your line and especially on the wire trace. Make up your own traces so that should one fail through sloppy workmanship you know exactly who to blame.

gently squeeze at each end with a pair of pliers or forceps, before trimming the end off (fig. 6C). Be very careful when squeezing on crimps. It is easy to fracture or even go right through them if you use excessive pressure.

Repeat these simple procedures at the other end of the trace to add a snap-type swivel for quick lure changing (fig. 7), and your trace is complete. Berkeley's snap swivels are the best type to use in all situations because they are guaranteed to take specific loads. They are available in dull black, and the size 10, which is perfect for all traces, has a loading of 50 lb. Though small, it is more than adequate. Berkeley cross-lok snap swivels are at least twice the price of others, but are infinitely superior. Sizes 7 or 5 are best for changing lures easily, especially when your fingers are cold. Fig. 7B shows a trace to which a plastic anti-kink vane has been added to alleviate line twist when using spinners.

To make a standard snap-tackle trace using a brace of trebles, follow exactly the procedure above, depending on the type of wire. For nearly all my pike fishing, I find size 8 hooks more than adequate. I even step down to size 10s if presenting small deadbaits such as sprats. I like the traces of my snap tackles to be 20 in long for a specific reason:

should the treble end become kinked or frayed, or one of the trebles badly bent through using forceps, I can snip it off and make it up again without even removing the trace from the rig, knowing that at worst it will be reduced to 15–16 in long, more than adequate for any pike. The wire simply passes through the eye of the up-trace treble, which can be held in any position (depending on bait size) by wrapping the wire carefully five times around the shank (as in fig. 7C).

When using very small livebaits, two trebles are not really necessary so make the trace up using a single size 8. That is the beauty of making your own traces. You can make them to your own design using the best quality trebles and swivels. And should one snap or fracture through sloppy workmanship, costing you a big fish, you know exactly who to blame.

A small kit containing swivels, hooks, crimps and wire fits into the smallest of boxes. Made-up traces ready for use are best kept individually wrapped in packets, or in a specialized container such as a trace tidy or a rig bin.

FLOATS

Pike float selection depends on whether you want to support the bait off bottom on a free-roaming or paternoster rig, drift it with the wind, suspend it with a

To ensure that through-the-middle sliding floats do not jam on the trace swivel, sleeve a bead on to the line between float and swivel.

FIGURE 8 *Pike floats*

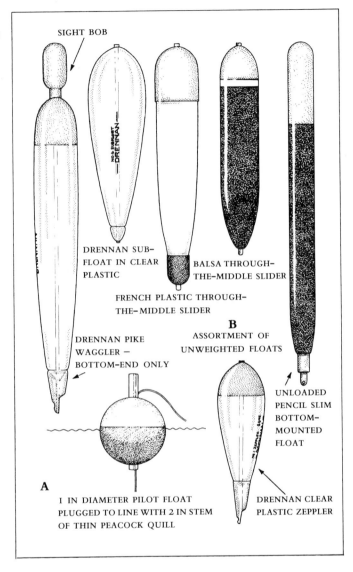

SIGHT BOB

DRENNAN SUB-
FLOAT IN CLEAR
PLASTIC

BALSA THROUGH-
THE-MIDDLE SLIDER

FRENCH PLASTIC THROUGH-
THE-MIDDLE SLIDER

B

DRENNAN PIKE
WAGGLER –
BOTTOM-END ONLY

ASSORTMENT OF
UNWEIGHTED FLOATS

UNLOADED
PENCIL SLIM
BOTTOM-
MOUNTED
FLOAT

A

1 IN DIAMETER PILOT FLOAT
PLUGGED TO LINE WITH 2 IN STEM
OF THIN PEACOCK QUILL

DRENNAN CLEAR
PLASTIC ZEPPLER

sunk float above bottom weed, or merely use the float as a
bite indicator when, for instance, presenting static deadbaits
and you prefer watching a float to other forms of
indicators.

Let us start with floats used for supporting deadbaits or
livebaits off bottom and as a visual indicator. Size, and the
resulting buoyancy, are most important because if too
large a float is used, the pike feels resistance and ejects the
bait. Moreover, when the pike sulks down on the bottom
having grabbed, say, a roach livebait, and submerges an

enormous, buoyant float that would perhaps be better sold as a navigational marker rather than as a pike float, every time the pike relaxes its grip for swallowing, the bait is immediately yanked away by the float rising back to the surface. So over-large floats not only inhibit runs from spooky pike, they prevent the bait from being turned.

My favourite float for close-range livebaiting is a 1 in diameter pilot float plugged gently to the line with 2 in of thin peacock quill (see fig. 8A). To most anglers this probably seems ridiculously small, because the bait actually submerges it every now and then. But that's the whole point. A small float allows baits up to, say, 6 to 7 in long to work naturally, attracting far more pike. Besides, you are in no doubt when the bait has been taken.

When supporting larger live- or deadbaits or fishing at longer range, there are numerous cigar-shaped pike floats to fit the bill (fig. 8B). The clear plastic zepplers and pikers made by Drennan are ideal, and are available in a variety of sizes to suit that of the bait. With a tube down the centre and a small eye at the base, they can be threaded on to the line or fixed bottom-end only as sliders or fixed floats.

For presenting a livebait above bottom weed, you

FIGURE 9 *Subsurface floats*

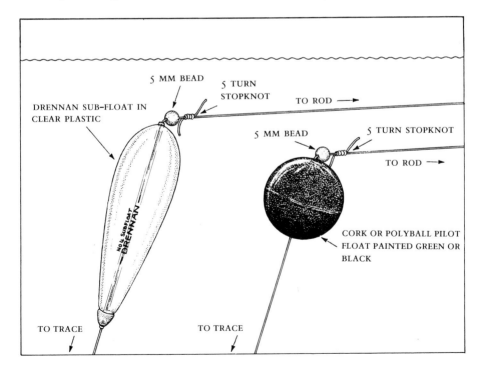

require what is called a 'sunken float' (fig. 9) such as the Drennan sub-float, which has a centre tube through which the line passes. Alternatively, a 1½- in diameter pilot float painted green or black will do at a pinch.

Loaded floats

For fishing deadbaits lying static on the bottom, when nothing needs supporting, the loaded or self-cocking float

FIGURE 10 *Loaded floats*

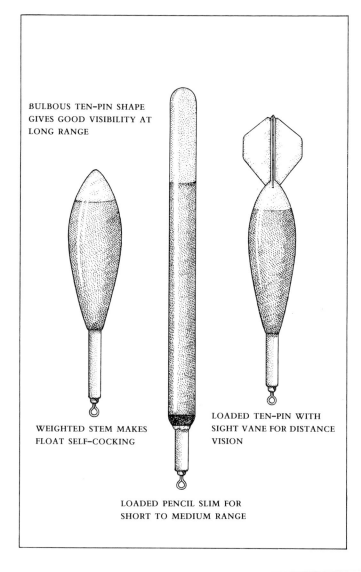

BULBOUS TEN-PIN SHAPE GIVES GOOD VISIBILITY AT LONG RANGE

WEIGHTED STEM MAKES FLOAT SELF-COCKING

LOADED TEN-PIN WITH SIGHT VANE FOR DISTANCE VISION

LOADED PENCIL SLIM FOR SHORT TO MEDIUM RANGE

is ideal. Like most other pike floats, these come in a range of shapes and sizes from pencil slims to the bulbous-topped ten-pin shape, depending on the range being fished and the subsequent visibility required (fig. 10).

For good visibility at a really long range, floats with sight-vanes pushed into the top are most useful, and add little extra buoyancy.

Drift floats

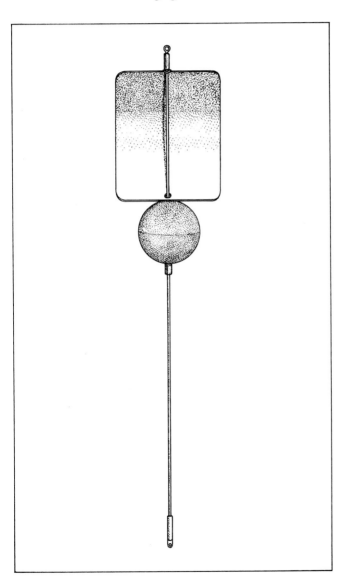

FIGURE 11 *ET drift-float*

For drifting both live- and deadbaits to far-off spots, beyond casting range, there are several sail-like drift floats available. The ET Drifter (fig. 11), for instance, has a long, counterbalancing wire stem going through the centre of a polyball body. The sail is then connected above the body and held in place with a rubber band. Spare sails in different colours to suit varying light conditions are available as extras.

INDICATORS

Drop-off/arm indicators

The simple drop-off or drop-arm indicator provides positive visual indication of a bite when ledgering, whether the pike moves off and away with the bait or swims directly towards the rod.

The unit consists of a plastic-covered steel needle with a flexible junction of silicone tubing, plus a terry clip at one end (for fixing to the rear rod rest) and a 1½-in diameter orange polyball and line clip at the other. Upon tightening up after casting, the bale arm is opened and the line is fixed into the line clip. When a pike runs towards the rod the arm drops back. And if the fish moves away, the arm lifts until the line pulls from the clip, whereupon the arm drops off and falls back – hence its name.

Drop-off indicators in both single and double models (for fishing two rods) also come fitted to electric alarm units, such as the ET Backbiter range, which provide a loud audible warning in addition to the visual indication of the arm itself.

Drop-off/Optonic bite alarm combos

Another way of combining the drop-off's excellent visibility with an audible warning is to use it in conjunction with an electric bite alarm as the front rod rest. The Optonic, for instance, can provide you with an excellent indication of the speed at which a pike is moving away with the bait.

Monkey climbers

Though not so efficient as the drop-off in visual terms, monkey climbers provide positive indications of bites, both away from and towards the rod. Used in conjunction with an electric alarm such as the Optonic, or even the old-fashioned antenna type, they are excellent for registering gentle takes, whether you are freelining or ledgering.

LANDING-NETS AND GLOVES

Because of the pike's length, a triangular net with arms measuring anywhere between 32 and 42 in, fitted with a deep mesh, is best. Such nets are kept rigid with the arms taut, or slightly bowed against the edges of the spreader block by a strong nylon cord which in effect becomes the front of the net. At a squeeze, even a 30-pounder would fold into a 32 in frame, but as the price difference between that and a 42 in net is marginal, it makes sense to be equipped with a net large enough to engulf easily any pike that comes along. And as a 20-pounder will measure approximately 40 in, the 42 in net is certainly none too large.

The net I have used for several years has lightweight 42 in hollow glass arms that bend easily into a pre-formed spreader block, and a deep, twin-mesh net. Even with a telescopic pole half extended, the frame is still reasonably manoeuvrable, and this is the yardstick by which large nets should be judged. With some really giant nets (50 in models are readily available), you may find it impossible to move the net towards the pike when you need to. Worse still, it may be impossible to raise the frame a few inches above the surface when the pike is inside once the mesh is fully soaked. So beware, and choose that net carefully.

The landing-net mesh itself is available in three different knotless nylon formats: straight, minnow-mesh sides with a nylon base; large-mesh sides with a micro base; or large-mesh sides with a soft, industrial-nylon base as used in carp and pike sacks. Each has been designed with the conservation of the pike in mind, and of the three the

A lightweight landing-net frame of 42 in hollow fibre glass arms is best. This can be quickly detached from the spreader block or un-screwed from the pole and hoisted straight on to the scales with the pike inside. Simply deduct the net's weight afterwards.

easiest to lift when wet is the large-mesh sides/micro base.

When choosing a net, make sure that it is deep enough for hoisting the pike on to the bank or into the boat simply by gripping the mesh around the middle in one hand and heaving. Also, with a deep mesh net, the pike does not have to be transferred to a specialist sling for weighing. Simply slip the frame from the spreader block, or unscrew the complete net and frame (depending upon the type), and hoist on to the scales. Once the pike has been returned, deduct the weight of the wet net and frame. This creates the minimum amount of stress to the pike.

In order to enjoy the freedom of wandering the bank with a lure rod, and even when bringing in a pike which has a flying treble or hooks on the outside of its jaws, I forget the net altogether. I simply slip a strong, rubberized, industrial-type glove (always in the back pocket of my fishing waistcoat or tackle bag) on to my left

hand and glove the pike out by the chin, unless both hooks
of the snap tackle or lure are visible on the outside, in
which case they can be flipped out easily with forceps and
the pike set free immediately – unless a trophy photo is
required.

GLOVING AND UNHOOKING

Provided care is taken, the technique of 'gloving' makes
hook removal a formality. It should be done with a glove
on the left hand (or the right hand if you are lefthanded).
You gently slip your fingers into the pike's left gill opening
and when half the hand is inside, clamp down against it
with your thumb (still on the outside) in a firm grip. The
pike may then be lifted safely from the water.

*By carefully inserting
a gloved left hand (if
you are right-handed)
into the pike's left gill
opening, a firm
purchase is obtained
for safe hook removal
using artery forceps,
thus avoiding the
pike's long, sharp
teeth.*

There is nothing macho about performing this with an unprotected hand, and suffering lacerated or bleeding knuckles from a brush with the pike's toothy gill filaments or secondary teeth on a freezing cold day, believe me – so glove up. Hardware shops stock a variety of suitable gloves.

When you are confident that your left-hand (or right-hand grip for lefthanders) grip is secure, lay the pike on its back on wet grass or a dampened unhooking mat (when boat-fishing I use a sheet of ½-in thick dense foam over the floorboards) and slowly curl your hand. The pike has no option then but to open its lower jaw. Then remove the hooks with long-nosed artery forceps from the front, or gently through the opposite gill slit if they are well back in the throat. Even really deeply hooked pike can be unhooked in this way (this is why semi-barbless hooks are so good), without the use of a gag or any other type of instrument, most of which can damage the fish's dentistry.

Forceps between 8 and 12 in long are ideal, and whatever you do don't be afraid of your pike. Treat it with firm respect.

SACKS AND TUBES

For retaining a specimen-sized pike until heavy rain stops falling or the light improves in order for a photo to be taken, use one of the specially designed sacks or tubes. These are made from strong, soft, industrial nylon, through which a series of holes have been punched allowing dissolved oxygen to permeate.

Remember to soak a keep-sack fully prior to popping the pike in or it will remove the fish's protective body slime, leaving it open to infection from disease or parasites. Then ease the sack with pike enclosed (the drawstring fully tightened) into a marginal depth of 1–2 ft, preferably away from the fishing area so it will lie undisturbed until photographed and released, and secure the cord to a bank stick or clump of reeds. Unfortunately, within a short space of time the pike will liven up and be nowhere near as easy to hold up for the camera as it was immediately after the fight. So wherever possible take that photo immediately after unhooking. You will look happier, and the pike will be caused the absolute minimum of handling stress.

ECHO SOUNDERS/ FISH FINDERS

For the serious pike angler who regularly fishes from a boat, electronic wizardry is a great help, particularly when exploring large, previously unfished sheets of water that would otherwise take weeks of work with a plummet and sliding float rig. A good outline of the bottom contours can easily be made in a day using even a simple echo-sounder, marking the depths in ink on a drawing of the fishery. Some say it is cheating. I say it is making the most of whatever is at your disposal, in order to maximize your enjoyment.

There are two types of echo-sounders, though both work on the principle of sending a signal through a transducer down to the bottom and back.

Echo-sounders

The now outdated 'Seafarer' type provides an accurate account of depths as the boat moves along, whether propelled by oars or engine. By adjusting the sensitivity knob, objects situated between the surface and bottom do sometimes show up on the read-out band, but I have never been able to differentiate which is which, whether fish, weed or rubbish.

Fish-finders

With modern hi-tech sounders, fish location has become a fine art and new, more sophisticated models are appearing every year. Indeed, American charter-boat skippers who troll the Great Lakes in search of salmon for instance, could not possibly operate in such vast waters without ultrasonic fish-finders. A vast multi-million dollar industry would crumble, as would commercial fishing as we know it

With the transducer clamped to the transom, even simple echo-sounders such as the Seafarer provide quick and accurate depth soundings of a new fishery, whether you row or use an outboard-engine. Hi-tec units such as the Humminbird show the fish in red above black bottom contours on the display screen.

today, for which such electronic sonar equipment was first developed.

The models I have used for several years now – whilst trolling for giant lake trout in Canada, locating the nile perch of Lake Victoria in Kenya, and of course for locating pike in the gravel pits, lakes and broads of Norfolk – are made by Humminbird. These fabulous units (other recommended finders are manufactured by Lowrance) operate by sending, through the transducer that clips on to the boat's transom with a suction pad, ultrasonic signals at 5000 cycles per second down to the bottom and back. The read-out appears on the TV-type screen as a black outline, showing the surface line and bottom contours.

The bottom, weed-beds and rocks show up in black and the fish show up as red squares, so there is never any question as to what is what. In addition, an alarm bleep is emitted as each fish or shoal comes up on the screen. The screen is calibrated vertically with a depth scale, so you know immediately at what depth the fish are situated.

This and numerous other features guarantee the fact that fish-finders are definitely here to stay, because they instantly put you right on top of the fish. However, you still need to catch them.

CHAPTER FIVE

BAITS
AND
LURES

A LTHOUGH pike eat all kinds of waterbound creatures, such as crayfish, worms, newts, frogs, toads and even fully grown waterbirds, as far as serious fishing is concerned baits fall into three distinct categories – live-baits, deadbaits and artificial lures.

LIVEBAITS

As there is nothing in the way of scales and fins that a pike will not eat, one might say that any small fish will suffice as a livebait. However, some species look better, work more attractively, and last considerably longer as an active bait than others.

Availability is the main consideration when it comes to choosing bait fish. As there is continual pressure on stocks of shoal fish from pollution, farming chemicals, years of poor fry recruitment owing to inconsistent weather patterns, and so on, the first question any conservation-minded fisherman must ask himself is a controversial one. Can the fishery that I catch bait fish from afford to lose a dozen or two small shoal fish in order to catch a pike or two which are then returned? Because sooner or later (and in small fisheries it takes but a couple of years) the delicate balance between predator and prey can be irreversibly upset. It is also wrong to ruin the enjoyment of float fishermen by removing all the small roach from a fishery for use as livebait. So only take livebaits if you are certain that it will not affect the sport of others.

Gudgeon and bleak

Both of these species attract pike well, the gudgeon because it is constantly on the move sending out distress signals to predators, and the bleak because of its highly reflective silver enamel colour. These are good close-range baits which, owing to their small size, invariably attract equally small pike. To encourage maximum manoeuvrability, present them on a single size 8 semi-barbless treble, hooked once only through the nostrils (fig. 12A).

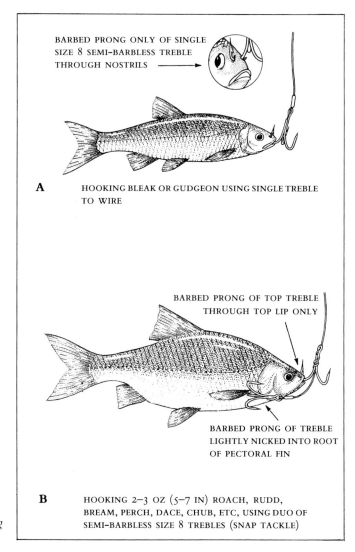

BARBED PRONG ONLY OF SINGLE
SIZE 8 SEMI–BARBLESS TREBLE
THROUGH NOSTRILS ———————→

A   HOOKING BLEAK OR GUDGEON USING SINGLE TREBLE
TO WIRE

BARBED PRONG OF TOP TREBLE
THROUGH TOP LIP ONLY

BARBED PRONG OF TREBLE
LIGHTLY NICKED INTO ROOT
OF PECTORAL FIN

B   HOOKING 2–3 OZ (5–7 IN) ROACH, RUDD,
BREAM, PERCH, DACE, CHUB, ETC, USING DUO OF
SEMI–BARBLESS SIZE 8 TREBLES (SNAP TACKLE)

FIGURE 12 *Hooking
livebaits*

Dace, rudd, roach, chub, bream and perch

Of these, the rudd is the best to use in shallow, weedy waters because it automatically works the upper water layers near the surface. The chub is probably the strongest of the group and lasts longer. There is no truth whatsoever in the old wive's tale that pike will not eat perch because of their spiky dorsal fin. Perch are gulped down greedily just like other small fish, and they make a fine, active bait. Apart from these considerations it is down to the local availability of each species, for I doubt the pike has a real preference. The ideal size for casting, controlling the bait, and for the ease with which they can be turned in the pike's jaws, are fish in the 5–7 in (2–3 oz) bracket. Really large livebaits are not only wasteful, but unnecessary. More runs are missed with large livebaits than for any other single reason, because small pike grab and subsequently make a mess of quality fish that they have little chance of swallowing.

Everyone has their pet method of presenting livebaits, and I am no exception. I believe that by inserting a duo of semi-barbless size 8 trebles as illustrated in fig. 12B (one in the top lip, the other in the pectoral root), the bait is allowed maximum freedom to roam; and when engulfed, at least one of the trebles is pointing in the right direction for positive hooking.

Crucian, common and mirror carp

Small, chunky carp in the 4–6 in range are very strong workers and will keep active for hours. A size 8 snap tackle suffices.

Trout

Rainbow trout for use as livebaits are readily available from fish farms. They come in various sizes, usually at very competitive prices. They are strong workers, and because their use does not affect the balance in coarse fisheries, they are perhaps the ideal livebait. Those 5–6 in long are nicely matched to a size 8 snap tackle.

*Hook small baits with
one prong of the
bottom treble in the
pectoral root and one
prong of the upper
hook in the top lip
(use semi-barbless
trebles) to ensure
maximum manouvr-
ability and attract
more pike.*

Fish movement

You must be sure to check the local river authority rules concerning the transfer of all bait fish from one water to another, whether trout from a farm, or cyprinid species caught from one river system for use in another. To be absolutely certain, catch your livebaits only from the water in which you are pike fishing. If this proves easy, at least you will have the comfort of knowing the fishery is prolific in shoal fish and can thus afford to part with some for pike baits.

DEADBAITS

Pike are certainly able to distinguish between freshly killed and long-term frozen baits. Their smell is totally different even to humans, and there is nothing more attractive or effective than a freshly killed deadbait. However, particularly during cold winter spells, we are not always permitted the luxury of catching and using small fish on the same day. You can ensure that they are at least as fresh as possible by tapping each on the head and wrapping it individually in cling film or a mini polybag and putting straight into the freezer. Baits which break down after a

couple of casts when wobbled, or disintegrate during a powerful distance cast, are useless.

It really is worth taking time and trouble to gather or purchase deadbaits and store them correctly. Freezing down a dozen or so fish in one lump all covered in slime and twigs and loosely wrapped in newspaper, for instance, apart from being sloppy, is a complete waste of good fish.

All of the cyprinid species mentioned under livebaits will catch pike when presented dead, either static or wobbled. My preference when wobbling is for a silver, firm-bodied fish like roach, rudd, dace, chub or rainbow trout, which are particularly tough. Small grayling can well withstand constant casting, but at the very head of the list for durability is the freshwater eel.

A comprehensive selection of deadbaits comprising both coloured and natural small freshwater and saltwater species, plus an oddity – squid – which is well worth trying.

Eels

In most river systems eels are easy to catch during the summer on maggots or worms. In my local Norfolk rivers they are a positive nuisance. But I do not object to setting out specifically to catch a few dozen for freezing down in readiness for winter use. If you do not fancy catching them, there is a ready source available wherever dragline dredgers are operating in lakes or rivers. Those clearing out rivers are more productive, even if only because the bottom silt is usually stacked up along the banks. It is then simply a matter of wading through the silt, sifting it for eels. If you can catch the dragline when it is actually working, so much the better. Within seconds of the shoe depositing its load on the bank, eels can be seen wriggling out all over the place. They can be found up to several days afterwards all along the heaps of silt where it has not dried off too much.

FIGURE 13 *Hooking eel deadbaits*

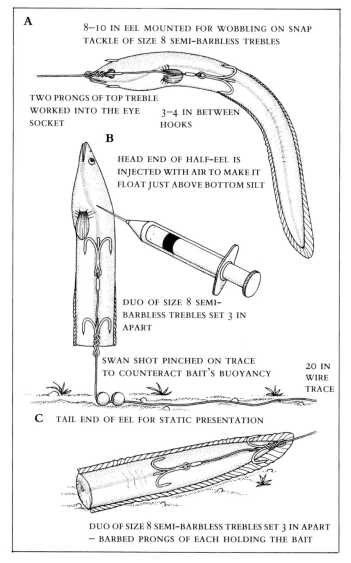

A

8–10 IN EEL MOUNTED FOR WOBBLING ON SNAP TACKLE OF SIZE 8 SEMI-BARBLESS TREBLES

TWO PRONGS OF TOP TREBLE WORKED INTO THE EYE SOCKET

3–4 IN BETWEEN HOOKS

B

HEAD END OF HALF-EEL IS INJECTED WITH AIR TO MAKE IT FLOAT JUST ABOVE BOTTOM SILT

DUO OF SIZE 8 SEMI-BARBLESS TREBLES SET 3 IN APART

SWAN SHOT PINCHED ON TRACE TO COUNTERACT BAIT'S BUOYANCY

20 IN WIRE TRACE

C   TAIL END OF EEL FOR STATIC PRESENTATION

DUO OF SIZE 8 SEMI-BARBLESS TREBLES SET 3 IN APART – BARBED PRONGS OF EACH HOLDING THE BAIT

Eels between 8 and 14 in long are perfect. The shorter ones are best used whole for wobbling. In fact, I have wobbled all day with just three or four eels, and taken several pike on each without the baits wearing down or breaking up. And they look so life-like if mounted with two prongs of the top treble worked into the eye socket and the bottom one set 3 in down the body (fig. 13A). Cut the longer eels in half for static presentation. Head or tail end? I am certain it matters little to the pike, at least not in my local waters where an enormous number of eels are consumed by them.

For a change, try offering the head end injected with air from a hypodermic syringe, or insert a length of foam strip so it rises tantalizingly out of the bottom silt (fig. 13B), with three or four swan shot midway along the trace to hold the eel down. This is a great way of ensuring that the bait rises above a silty bottom or blanket weed where non-buoyant baits could become hidden from the pike's view. The tail end is best offered lying static on the bottom, rigged as in fig. 13C.

Eels are a fabulous natural bait, free, and you can take as many as you like without upsetting anyone, or anyone else's fishing.

Seafish

Owing to their pungent and most distinctive smell, many species of seafish make excellent deadbaits. The effectiveness of sprats, herrings and mackerel, for instance, is well known. If fishing a water where the pike rarely see the angler's bait, I would still put my faith in a fresh herring above all else. On the fishmonger's slab, look for the bright red eye and crimson gill filaments, and those golden scales that easily come away from the flanks (when the bait hits the water) and scatter down in a shower of stardust to settle all around the bottom. What could possibly be more attractive to a foraging pike?

In addition to being wobbled on light tackle (a size 10 snap tackle is ideal), sprats are great to use as a loose-feed attractor. Try chopping a few into halves or quarters and scatter around a larger deadbait presented static on the bottom.

To raise the head of a static deadbait tantalizingly off the bottom, inject a little air into its shoulder with a hypodermic syringe, remembering to add sufficient swan shots to the trace to counteract its buoyancy.

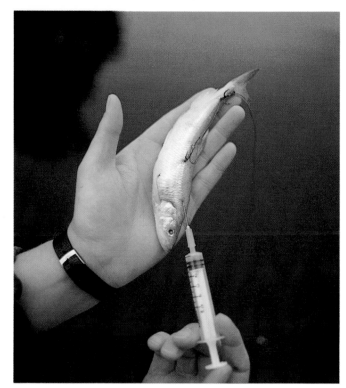

When fresh, the herring is arguably the most attractive deadbait of them all. When it is cut in half diagonally, the oily juices permeate the water much more quickly than whole baits. The heads are just as effective as the tail ends.

Probably the all-time favourite is the half-mackerel, or
to be more precise the mackerel tail. It should be presented
on a duo of size 8 or 6 trebles, with the uppermost one
worked into the sinewy muscles of the narrow tail root,
and the bottom one 3 in away (fig. 14).

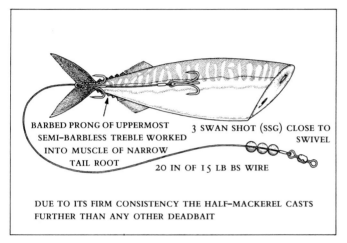

FIGURE 14 *Mackerel
tail*

BARBED PRONG OF UPPERMOST   3 SWAN SHOT (SSG) CLOSE TO
SEMI–BARBLESS TREBLE WORKED   SWIVEL
INTO MUSCLE OF NARROW
TAIL ROOT   20 IN OF 15 LB BS WIRE

DUE TO ITS FIRM CONSISTENCY THE HALF–MACKEREL CASTS
FURTHER THAN ANY OTHER DEADBAIT

The half-mackerel will cast further than any other
deadbait, and for stillwater fishing there is no need to add
extra lead, in the way of bombs, to the line. Simply pinch
three swan shot on to the trace immediately below the
swivel to give the pike a little something to pull against. In
recent years, pike fishermen have discovered that almost
any small seafish will catch pike and this opens up an
exciting new field. You can offer alternative or change
baits to spooky pike regularly caught on deadbaits, just as
the carp fisherman does.

Durable seafish that are particularly firm in the body,
and thus best suited to wobbling, are small 'joey' mackerel,
scad (horse mackerel), red gurnard and mullet. I also like
the cucumber-smelling smelt for wobbling. It is readily
available in flat freezer packs from most tackle dealers,
although this fish does tend to break up rather easily.

Smelt are better as a static bait because, owing to their
distinct aroma, they are great attractors. Other softish
deadbaits that are best offered as statics are sardines and
sand eels. As I mentioned previously, any odd-looking
seafish which appears on the fishmonger's slab is certainly
worth trying, especially brightly coloured species originat-

ing from the Mediterranean area, such as giltheads and red bream.

Oddities

Other oddities from the sea that are well worth trying, especially in hard-fished waters where the pike probably know the names of the species used to catch them better than fishermen, are baby octopus and squid. Presented static (very tiny squid can be electric when wobbled) just like a herring, these really do produce.

A friend of mine has achieved no small measure of success in recent years with uncooked turkey pieces. Yes – turkey pieces. Working in a turkey processing factory, he has access to scrap chunks and these in the coloured waters of the Norfolk Broads are regularly snapped up from the bottom when presented static. Pike obviously recognize a mouthful of good, wholesome food on the bottom and swallow it. After all, pike eat ducklings and the body of a duckling without feathers is not so different from a chunk of turkey.

Even a small, dead rodent, a rat, mole or mouse found by the waterside, is worth a try so long as it is fresh. So be prepared to keep a very open mind.

Colouring deadbaits

For added attraction, especially on waters that receive regular attention, colouring any of the previously mentioned deadbaits can produce interesting results. There is no doubt that under certain conditions, baits coloured red, gold, blue, yellow or even green, show up surprisingly well compared to the fish's natural colour. And pike can show a marked preference for a certain colour when it suits them.

Deadbaits can be coloured easily using either neat liquid food colouring or the powder dyes used for making carp baits. Neat food colouring straight from the bottle can be applied by brushing it on both sides of the fish and leaving it to dry. Prior to brushing the colour on, be sure to blot off excess water with a piece of kitchen roll. Powder dyes are used by adding a spoonful of dye to half a cup of water and mixing in a shallow dish or 2 pt bait tin. It can be brushed on, or the bait's tail can be gripped in a pair of locking artery forceps so it can be swished slowly around until both sides are evenly covered.

Finally, wrap the coloured baits carefully in cling film and store in the freezer. When fishing in coloured water with a green tinge, deep yellow takes some beating, while overall, and especially in clear waters, red or deep gold are my favourites. The choice, however, is yours.

ARTIFICIAL LURES

An artificial lure is something which, when pulled through the water, irritates the pike into attacking and grabbing it, through hunger, territorial aggression or just because it feels so inclined. Lures are constructed from metal, wood, rubber, plastic, feathers or fur and fitted with large single, treble or even multi-treble hooks. Some are heavily weighted, others are buoyant, while many combine the action of floating and diving through built-in alloy or plastic vanes. Some are drilled with holes for water to gurgle through, whilst others have an inbuilt rattle from a chamber containing a ball-bearing. Some have propellors to churn the surface, and some are fitted with flapping arms. Lures are designed to throb, gurgle, nose-dive, deep-dive, wriggle, jig, flap, sink slowly, float upwards slowly, dive fast, vibrate, twitch, rattle, pop and pulsate. The weedless varieties may even be confidently retrieved through thick weed-beds. There are even battery operated electric lures whose eyes light up for night-time fishing, or which swim about all by themselves.

Artificial lures are manufactured in just about every conceivable colour combination known to modern man and might resemble anything from a household spoon to a live frog. They offer the inventor more scope than any other single item of fishing tackle. Moreover, when it seems that everything has been tried already, out comes yet another new plug or spinner bait in yet another format. And fishermen will always have more trouble resisting them than the pike they are intended to deceive.

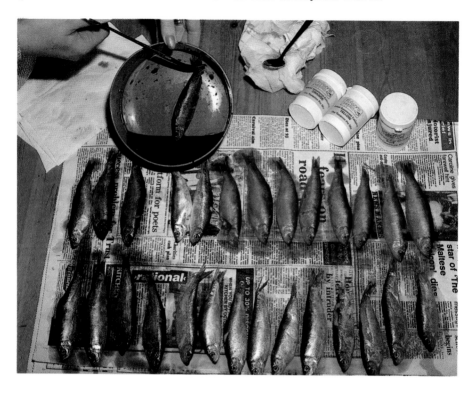

To colour deadbaits, first blot off excess water with newspaper. These deadbaits have been coloured with some powder dyes that are used for making carp baits. Grip the fish's tail with forceps and swish it around until the colour is even.

This is not to say, as many indeed think, that lures are made purely to fool fishermen. Each has a very special part to play through its unique and individual action, and the fun of catching pike with artificial lures lies in trying them all so you know what each is capable of doing, the depth to which it works and the speed at which it can be retrieved. You will then have an answer to match whatever mood the pike is in, regardless of the depth at which it lies.

There are in fact so many thousands of different artificial lures available today from patterns old and new, split up into several different categories, that it is impossible to list them all, but the following selection should give the pike angler a more than reasonable armoury. To start with, let us return to where it might have begun, to the ordinary, yet deadly 'spoon'. This is my own standby wherever I find myself pike fishing in a new water or different country. In recent years I have made several trips to Canada to fish the cold sweet-water lakes of Manitoba and the North West Territories for lake trout and pike. Without question, and for both species incidentally, the most effective lure proved to be the spoon.

Correct choice of artificial lure from the tackle dealer's wall is imperative. Each has been designed to work in a particular way and within a specific depth band.

Spoons

Made from hammered copper sheeting, brass, chrome plated steel, aluminium, even heavy plastic, the spoon usually comes fitted with a treble at one end and a swivel at the other, both joined by split rings. It is great fun to make your own by buying up a bundle of old spoons of various sizes at car boot or jumble sales, cutting off the handles and drilling a hole at each end, to which the swivel and treble are joined by split rings. For the outlay of a few pounds you can make dozens and dozens of different spoons in a variety of sizes and shapes.

Because of its weight, the spoon is great for casting into the wind and can even be used as a plummet, employing the count-down method of allowing one second per foot of descent from the moment it hits surface until the line goes limp when the spoon touches bottom.

As it does not spin, but wiggles or wobbles from side to side against the water pressure, there is no need for an anti-kink vane, because spoons do not create line twist. They can therefore be retrieved at almost any speed. For coloured water, a slow retrieve allows time for the pike to home in and grab; whereas in extremely clear water, pike are loath to follow unless the pace is fast and variable. It is as though they enjoy the chase. The spoon shape is roughly oval, although bar types are decidedly more elongated.

Lengths of 3–6 inches suffice for most situations, although for trolling huge lochs or loughs spoons of up to 10 in long are necessary. These may appear large, but what is a 10 in fish to a 20 lb pike.

One of the most effective spoon shapes is the bar type or ABU Toby, which incorporates angled fins at the rear and is available in numerous lengths from 2 to 6 in and from 10 to 40 grams. I also love ABU's Atom, a deep-sided, ribbed spoon that has a red plastic teaser attached to the split ring of the treble, and the UTO, a large, unique spoon that has a treble fitted at both ends.

Other favourites of mine among the large spoons are the Storauren made by Solvkroken. These have numerous holes drilled along the edges to secure the treble in varying positions or to facilitate fitting extra trebles; the Kuusamo Professor, which has a tantalizing flapping action; and the original 'Red Eye', a deep-bodied, highly polished silver spoon incorporating reflective eyes.

Of the weedless varieties, the ABU Favourite and the Dardevle weedless are terrific, and come fitted with sprung wire guards that protect the large single hooks from catching on aquatic vegetation no matter how thick.

As for colour, I tend to be rather old fashioned, preferring plain gold, brass or silver. Combinations of coloured spots, stripes, even two tones, will have their day so it pays to carry a variety. Much of the spoon's attraction emanates from its reflective 'flash pattern', so don't allow the surface to tarnish. Keep a small tin of metal polish handy and regularly buff your spoons up with a piece of cloth. It makes all the difference, believe me.

Spinners

These vibratory lures differ from spoons in that the blade or spoon revolves around a weighted bar or stem, to which the hook is connected. To alleviate line twist, you need to incorporate a plastic anti-kink vane when making a 10 in wire spinning trace.

Spinners such as the Voblex, which is a fabulous lure in the larger sizes, are unique because the rubbery head in front of the blade acts as a built-in anti-kink device. The American 'Dardevle' spinners made by Eppinger overcome line twist in a most simple way. The wire stem for a distance of ⅜ in in front of the blade is bent almost at right angles.

Spinners attract pike because they emit tantalizing vibratory pulses or buzz while 'flashing', as though a small fish is passing by. Most are of the blade type – an oval or heart-shaped blade spins at high speed around the shaft. Brass or silver collars, brightly coloured beads, deer hair, plastic skirts, feathers and even latex rubber help to stir the pike's predatory nature, as in the Flying C made by the Kilty Lure Co. Better known as the 'flying condom', this large spinner incorporates a long, oval blade, revolving around a long shaft covered in thick latex available in several colours. This spinner is a hit with salmon anglers because, owing to its long shaft, it hooks well, and I have used it most successfully for pike.

Old standbys like the Colorado and Kidney, heavily chromed spoons that are spinners because their blades revolve, still catch pike, but are not so popular today due to the enormous choice now available from Sweden, Canada, Finland, France and, of course, the home of artificial lures, the USA.

A proportion of pike fishermen still stay true to the well-proven makes of spinners such as the 'Mepps' and Ondex, ABU's 'Droppen', and even the Devon minnow which, although considered a salmon lure, does catch a lot of pike. Devons are available in metal for deep-lying fish in heavy water, and in wood for a buoyant retrieve just off bottom. For this an up-trace lead is incorporated. The lead, not the lure, bumps over the bottom; the lure spins attractively above it, missing all the rocks and other snags.

John unhooks a summer weir-pool pike which obviously had a liking for the fluttering action of ABU's 'atom', a ribbed, deep-sided spoon.

Spinner baits

Although spinner baits are an American invention, evolved from spoons and spinners for the downfall of the large-mouth bass and other sunfishes, in certain situations – heavily coloured water in particular, where visibility is minimal – they are fantastic pike catchers. This is due to the tremendous vibrations emitted from the large single or two small blades connected to the top of the v-shaped shaft. At the bottom of the shaft, behind a leaded head, is attached a large single hook inside a pulsating, squid-like plastic skirt. Both blades and skirts are interchangeable, and available in a galaxy of colours, and the skirt helps to make this lure quite weed-free. Two spinner baits in particular are recommended, Barries Buzzer and Double Buzzer made by Ryobi Masterline.

A box large enough to hold one of each type of artificial lure available has not yet been made. This selection includes both the vibratory spinner baits and buzz baits. These, although originally designed to attract black bass, score well with pike, especially in low visibility.

Unfortunately, the large single hook is nowhere near so successful for hooking pike as for black bass, and I always wire on a size 6 treble to the bend of the single. This converts a much higher proportion of 'hits' into pike on the bank, although the additional treble does ruin the lure's weed-free properties.

There are numerous variations of the spinner bait in a whole range of sizes; some even come fitted with latex rubber fish as opposed to the skirt. Those which incorporate a lead-headed jig with a sleeve-on plastic worm are particularly effective and great fun to use on a light outfit.

Buzz baits

These are top-water lures with a similar v-shaped but much shorter top shaft than spinner baits. They also

incorporate a propeller, which churns the surface film.
Some come fitted with double, opposite-rotating propeller
blades creating massive surface displacement – guaranteed
to bring even deaf pike out of the weeds and up to the top
for an attack. And that is the secret of buzz baits, pike just
cannot resist their irritating audacity. I particularly like
Eppinger's Buzz 'n' Devle, which incorporates a spoon
and weedless hook. It can be yanked through the toughest
surface vegetation without hang-ups, and produces the
most glorious, spectacular attacks.

Plugs

Lastly, we come to all those marvellous creations in wood,
high-density plastic, nylon, aluminium and copper known
as plugs. There are several different types, but for
convenience sake I shall group them as floaters, floating
divers, and sinkers that dive, because the ability to identify
each type and understand how it works provides the secret
to catching pike on plugs.

Floaters

Pure surface floaters or 'poppers' are great for bringing the
pike out of or away from its cover and up to the surface for
an attack. They stimulate interest in the thickest covering
of surface plants, such as lilies, by the way they gurgle,
plop and splutter. The best-known surface plug is the
Heddon Crazy Crawler which, by means of its hinged
arms that are activated by the retrieve, flip-flaps like a
swimmer doing butterfly stroke. One of my favourites,
also made by Heddon, is the Torpedo, which is equipped
with churning propellers at both front and rear. Worked in
short, sharp pulls, this lure really gets the pike hopping
made. The Creek Chub mouse, which sports a stiff bushy
tail, is another firm favourite.

For a splashy, snag-free retrieve, insist on floaters that
have hooks protected by thin wire weed-guards. Most
good makes have them fitted. Surface plugs are among the
most exciting to use because you not only anticipate the
savage take, you also see it. Incidentally, it is not difficult

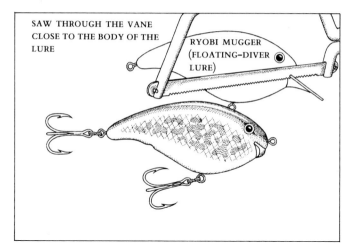

SAW THROUGH THE VANE
CLOSE TO THE BODY OF THE
LURE

RYOBI MUGGER
(FLOATING-DIVER
LURE)

FIGURE 15 *Adapting
a floating-diver to a
floater*

to convert floating divers such as Ryobi's Mugger or
Shakespeare's Big S range into pure floaters that simply
pop and gurgle. Saw gently through the diving lip using a
fine-tooth hacksaw and gently rub in a drop of rapid, hard-
setting waterproof glue to fill in and smooth over (fig. 15).
Any single or double-jointed floating diver can be doctored
in this way if your pike fishing demands a greater selection
of floaters than is available from the local tackle shop.

Floating divers

These extremely versatile plugs float and gurgle when
pulled gently, but then dive when the retrieve is stepped up
due to the angled vane or lip under the chin. They come in
all sorts of shapes and sizes, in both single and double-
jointed formats. The faster you retrieve, the deeper they
dive; and whenever you pause during the retrieve, the plug
starts to float back up to the surface.

There is an easy way of telling whether a particular
model has been designed for shallow or deep diving, and
this is by the size of the diving vane. Those with enormous
lips such as Bill Norman's Deep Big N, Heddon's Timber
Rattler or the Kwikfish King Kranky, can be quickly
cranked down to 10 ft or more. In fact, the term 'crank
bait' is the apt American name given to floaters which dive
deep when being retrieved fast.

Floating divers that contain a steel ball-bearing inside a

Floating divers that contain ball-bearing rattlers inside appeal to the pike's vibratory senses and are among the most effective of all artificial lures.

hollow chamber, and thus rattle and emit sound waves, are the most effective within this range. The Ryobi Mugger and Shakespeare's Big S range are both well proven pike catchers, as are Rapala's Shad Rap and the Shad Rattler from Mirrolure. An unusual plug, in that its tiny vibratory blade protrudes from its rear, is the famous Heddon Big Bud, which only dives a few feet but really does bring out the worst in pike. They just have to attack it.

Looking exactly as its name implies, the Meadow Mouse, also from Heddon, is another shallow but extremely attractive floating diver which turns pike wild.

Helin's 'flat fish' lures, the laziest of floating divers, can be retrieved extremely slowly due to their 'distinct' banana shape, which creates enormous water resistance. They are therefore particularly suited to coloured water and for pike that need time to home in on their food.

Lastly, because this plug has been catching pike since it was first created over 50 years ago, Heddon's River Runt has a great diving action for both slow-jerking retrieves or dives down to 8 ft.

Genuine American-made lures may cost substantially more than imitations from the Far East, but their superior action is what catches pike.

There are occasions when a particular colour does produce over all others on the day. Fluorescent pink is a firm favourite of the author for working shallow, clear waters.

Sinking plugs that dive

Plugs that sink by themselves can be counted down towards the bottom at a rate of roughly one second per foot of descent, just like big spoons, so in effect they help you to plummet the depth as you fish. Some have rattles for extra attraction, and most come fitted with much smaller vanes or lips than floating divers because their weight is enough to take them down to the desired fishing depth. They will then dive a few extra feet when retrieved. These plugs are great for reaching pike lying close to the bottom in really deep water beyond the comfortable depth workable with floating divers, say depths well in excess of 10–12 ft.

Rapala's Magnum sinking plugs are considered to be the

finest lures available, especially suited to trolling. They are strongly built with good-quality trebles and come in a variety of weights and metallic colour combinations, with body lengths up to 7 in. For general work, Rapala's countdown sinking and double-jointed sinking plugs are really great. ABU make superb sinking plugs too, and I particularly recommend the Killer balsa sinkers, which come in a variety of colours in both single and double-jointed formats, up to 20 grams in weight and 6 in in length.

The 40 gram Killer Magnum sinker (a blue-water, offshore lure really) happens also to be a great deep-water pike lure for casting or trolling. A most exciting range, sporting highly reflective, mirror-like bodies, including both single and double-jointed versions, is made by the Japanese company Yo Zuri.

Colour

I have left the question of colour until last because in most situations I believe a lure is taken because of its shape and the tantalizing action it creates. But there are times when a particular colour does without question produce fish in a specific situation, so it is wise to have an extensive collection. My favourite 'single' colours for plugs are silver, gold and fluorescent pink, with red and white, imitation 'perch' and blue mackerel heading the list of 'combination' colours. I also like plain silver, brass, copper or gold when choosing spoons and spinners, and invariably try these first, keeping in reserve a whole bunch of coloured variations, two-tone, spotted and striped. At the end of the day, however, it is probably a matter of confidence, and I always first consider the lure's size, its weight and its action before colour.

CHAPTER SIX

TECHNIQUES AND RIGS

LIVEBAITING

There is good reason why using livebait to catch pike is so effective. By offering the pike an exact part of its daily diet – live fish – the presentation arouses far less suspicion and caution when the pike grabs hold, compared, say, to chomping on something alien and metallic such as an artificial lure, or even a wobbled deadbait that does not try to get away.

Pike that inhabit really hard-fished, clear waters, for instance, sometimes make you believe that unless a live fish is offered you may as well go home. However, as my own pike fishing moves further away from livebaiting (as it has done these last ten years, increasingly influenced by deadbaiting techniques and the use of artificial lures) such situations arise less and less often. What matters most is that you have confidence in the technique you are using and in your own ability.

Of course livebaiting is not the panacea to catching pike with ease if the bait is presented unattractively. Pike do not automatically grab hold of a livebait simply because it is alive. The bait must be allowed to swim freely and appear to be evading the pike's jaws, or it could be ignored, or at best grabbed momentarily and then dropped. Those huge, cork, pike bungs of yesteryear called the 'Gazette' for instance, probably accounted for more missed runs, because the pike dropped the bait upon feeling undue resistance, than ever were caught by using them. We credit all other species with the ability to feel resistance upon mouthing the bait, and use sensitive float rigs accordingly, so why not with pike.

Fortunately most modern pike floats are noticeably streamlined, allowing the bait to work freely and appear untethered, thus attracting more pike. Subsequently, when the pike decides to turn the bait for swallowing, it is not pulled from its jaws through an excessively buoyant float (see p. 48).

(see p. 48).

FLOAT-FISHED 'FREE-ROAMING' LIVEBAITS

Close-range rig

A considerably younger Wilson ponders the size of this River Wensum beauty which accepted a free-roving livebait trotted down a deep run in the upper reaches of Norfolk's River Wensum.

As can be seen from fig. 16A, my float rig for close-range free-roaming livebaiting is simplicity itself, incorporating one or two swan shot on the trace to keep the bait down, and a 1-in diameter pilot float plugged to the line with a thin, 2 in stem of peacock quill.

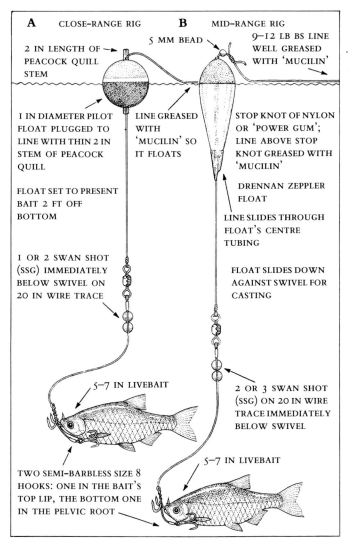

A   CLOSE-RANGE RIG   B   MID-RANGE RIG

2 IN LENGTH OF PEACOCK QUILL STEM

5 MM BEAD

9-12 LB BS LINE WELL GREASED WITH 'MUCILIN'

I IN DIAMETER PILOT FLOAT PLUGGED TO LINE WITH THIN 2 IN STEM OF PEACOCK QUILL

LINE GREASED WITH 'MUCILIN' SO IT FLOATS

STOP KNOT OF NYLON OR 'POWER GUM'; LINE ABOVE STOP KNOT GREASED WITH 'MUCILIN'

FLOAT SET TO PRESENT BAIT 2 FT OFF BOTTOM

DRENNAN ZEPPLER FLOAT

LINE SLIDES THROUGH FLOAT'S CENTRE TUBING

I OR 2 SWAN SHOT (SSG) IMMEDIATELY BELOW SWIVEL ON 20 IN WIRE TRACE

FLOAT SLIDES DOWN AGAINST SWIVEL FOR CASTING

5-7 IN LIVEBAIT

2 OR 3 SWAN SHOT (SSG) ON 20 IN WIRE TRACE IMMEDIATELY BELOW SWIVEL

5-7 IN LIVEBAIT

TWO SEMI-BARBLESS SIZE 8 HOOKS: ONE IN THE BAIT'S TOP LIP, THE BOTTOM ONE IN THE PELVIC ROOT

FIGURE 16 *Float-fished free-roaming livebaits for still or running water*

It is well worth taking time to grease the line above the float for 20–30 yd with solid mucilin (available in tins complete with felt applicator pad), to stop the line from sinking between rod tip and float. Otherwise, the bait's movements are hampered and it immediately becomes far less attractive. Apart from which, striking becomes impaired when the line is heavily sunk. But with the line floating nicely on the surface film, even small (5–7 in) livebaits can be encouraged to work long distances, and thus present themselves to pike over a greater area in either still or running water.

Because by its nature I consider free-roaming livebaiting to be a truly roving technique, I usually prefer to hold the rod in order to 'work' the bait, encouraging it to swim wherever I suspect pike might be lying. For instance, gentle pressure against the bait invariably encourages it to swim off in the opposite direction, so the bale arm is left open with just a gentle pressure against the spool with the forefinger. And whenever the line forms into a huge bow due to the bait's movement, current or wind direction, it is a simple matter (because it is well greased) to lift the line from the water without affecting the bait's direction and to straighten it.

Consider the typical pike river in fig. 17, for instance, where, due to careful use of the flow pattern to trot the bait downstream over choice lies, and delicate float control to veer it across the flow before retrieving slowly and trotting down again, every pike has an opportunity to see the bait. Only one actual cast has been made, minimizing disturb- ance and maximizing the bait's freshness and strength, whereas continual casting would soon sap the bait's capacity to work.

FIGURE 17 On small to medium rivers, maximize the area covered by each cast in order to preserve the livebait's strength and will to work

In small to medium-sized rivers, pike (especially the larger, craftier ones) often succumb during that first all-

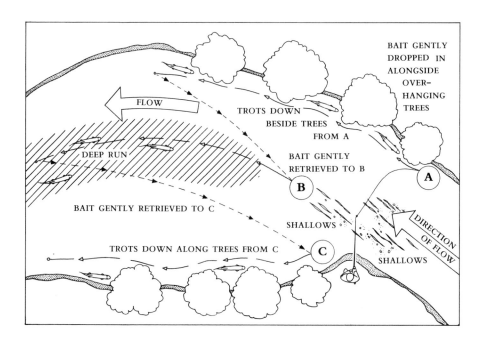

important cast and trot through, provided the bait is set at an acceptable depth beneath the float, say 2 ft off bottom. When pike have learnt to associate the disturbance caused by an angler with danger, the chance of success diminishes with each successive cast.

It goes without saying, of course, that a careful approach up to the water is very important. Pretend you are chub fishing and show the pike equal respect. It is no less sensitive than other species even though it owns a mouthful of sharp teeth. Its sensory organs, eyesight and built-in radar are second to none. For this reason, don't crunch up to the swim and whack the bait out as far as you can. Distance fishing does have its place, but pike by nature tend to occupy lies close into the bank beneath trees, in gaps between thick reed-beds, and so on. Always explore these first by standing well back from the edge and gently plopping the bait in only a few yards out. Then work areas further out.

Striking

A few lines are in order at this stage about that age-old problem, when is the best time to strike a pike that has taken a livebait, because they do tend to hang on tightly, even to relatively small baits. Whereas with static deadbaits, the pike seems to know it is not going to put up a fight and invariably sucks it straight back for swallowing.

With artificial lures you are compelled to strike immediately, quicker than the pike can eject it. But with livebaits a decision has to be made, and I am of the view that it is always better to strike early than late. To miss a small pike through striking prematurely is infinitely better than to deeply hook a big pike that has totally gorged the bait. And there is no way of telling what size of predator has grabbed your livebait. Adopt the view that if the hook comes unstuck on the strike or on the way in, the fish probably was not worth catching anyway. You will then suffer few deeply hooked fish.

The beauty of presenting relatively small livebaits is that as soon as the float goes positively under and away (often accompanied by a glorious swirl in shallow swims), you can close the bale arm and tighten down until the weight of the fish is felt, and then lean the rod back powerfully into a full bend and firm strike. Don't allow the rod tip to straighten at any time because when the pike senses danger it will open its jaws and shake its head from side to side in an effort to ditch the bait. Keep the rod well bent and continue winding so that when the bait does move, the hooks will be pulled home. Bear in mind that until the pike opens its jaws it is impossible for the hooks to catch hold, so tightly does it hold the bait.

When temperatures are low take along a small, fine-meshed aquarium net so that you do not have to search with your hands for a fresh livebait in freezing cold water. Its price more than compensates for the alternative of painfully cold hands.

Medium-range rig

For presenting the bait at greater depths or distances in stillwaters, or deep down close to the bottom of medium-paced rivers, an additional swan shot or two must be added to the trace, and this necessitates a larger float such as a

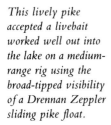

This lively pike accepted a livebait worked well out into the lake on a medium-range rig using the broad-tipped visibility of a Drennan Zeppler sliding pike float.

Drennan Zeppler, which is available in various sizes up to 30 grams.

To stop the float at the desired depth a bead is threaded on (before the float), and a five-turn stop knot tied above it at the desired depth using a few inches of reel line (see p. 41) or power gum. The line is threaded through the float's centre so it in effect becomes a slider, capable of presenting the bait at any depth. Simply wet the line and pull the stop knot up or down (see the mid-range rig in fig. 16B).

This is a good hooking rig too (as with all sliders) because the line passes freely through the float on the strike, whereas the 'fixed' float creates an unacceptable degree of water resistance with anything larger than the inch-diameter pilot float. For presenting livebaits at great distances, there is nothing more effective than the drift-float rig (see p. 109).

RUNNING PATERNOSTER LIVEBAIT RIG

Occasions will arise when the free-roaming livebait has less effect and you need to keep the bait in one spot. This happens when the water is well coloured, as in poor visibility the pike needs more than the usual amount of time to home in on the livebait. Free-roaming livebaits can even outrun a pike in heavily coloured water, and so the running paternoster rig is used (fig. 18). This rig is also effective during extremely low water temperatures, when pike are liable to be considerably more lethargic. Again, presentation of the bait in one spot allows the pike time to investigate its movements. Alternatively, you may wish to anchor the bait in the middle of a deep hole on the bend of a river where continually trotting a free-roaming bait proves unsuccessful; or to present it during windy conditions at various points along a deep gully in a gravel pit or lake without continually having to recast, as you would a free-roaming livebait.

As you can see from fig. 18A, the running paternoster is simple to construct, using the sliding float as a built-in plummet. For instance, if after casting out and tightening

FIGURE 18 *Running*
paternoster livebait rig

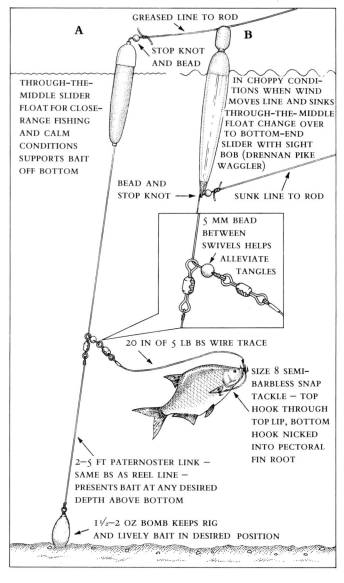

FIGURE 18 *Running paternoster livebait rig*

GREASED LINE TO ROD

A

B

STOP KNOT
AND BEAD

THROUGH–THE–
MIDDLE SLIDER
FLOAT FOR CLOSE–
RANGE FISHING
AND CALM
CONDITIONS
SUPPORTS BAIT
OFF BOTTOM

IN CHOPPY CONDI-
TIONS WHEN WIND
MOVES LINE AND SINKS
THROUGH–THE- MIDDLE
FLOAT CHANGE OVER
TO BOTTOM–END
SLIDER WITH SIGHT
BOB (DRENNAN PIKE
WAGGLER)

BEAD AND
STOP KNOT →

SUNK LINE TO ROD

5 MM BEAD
BETWEEN
SWIVELS HELPS
ALLEVIATE
TANGLES

20 IN OF 5 LB BS WIRE TRACE

SIZE 8 SEMI-
BARBLESS SNAP
TACKLE – TOP
HOOK THROUGH
TOP LIP, BOTTOM
HOOK NICKED
INTO PECTORAL
FIN ROOT

2–5 FT PATERNOSTER LINK –
SAME BS AS REEL LINE –
PRESENTS BAIT AT ANY DESIRED
DEPTH ABOVE BOTTOM

1½–2 OZ BOMB KEEPS RIG
AND LIVELY BAIT IN DESIRED POSITION

up gently the float lies flat, it has been set too deep. And if
it is taken beneath the surface it has been set too shallow.
Ideally it should be set slightly deeper than the swim so
that after tightening it remains upright and gently 'knocking'
to the movements of the livebait. In case a violent, long
run develops I like to fish with the bale arm open and a
loop of line lightly clipped beneath a run clip or an elastic
band situated around the handle immediately above the
reel. A pike can then pull the loop free and take line from

the open spool, but the livebait cannot. It is a simple yet effective ruse which works best with the rod set on two rests with the tip pointing at the float and angled upwards.

When fishing at distance or in strong winds, it is impossible to present a float-paternostered livebait with a greased line and through-the-middle slider. The wind bows the line and eventually pulls the rig away from the desired position. So you simply exchange the 'through-the-middle slider' for a bottom-only slider (such as the Drennan waggler pike float, which has an easily visible sight bob on the tip) and sink the line after casting – just as though you were roach fishing using a waggler float (as in fig. 18B), because exactly the same principles are involved. To ensure the line sinks quickly, keep a small bottle of neat washing-up liquid handy and dab a fingerful around the spool prior to casting. The bait can be presented at any depth from 2 ft off bottom upwards depending upon the length of the paternoster bomb link; you should allow for dense bottom weed or snags, and take into account pike that may be feeding among fry shoals, for instance, at mid-water. So increase or decrease the bomb link accordingly.

Before making each new cast and repositioning the bait, always make a point of inspecting the wire trace to ensure that constant bait movement has not kinked the wire. Badly kinked traces could easily fracture at the wrong moment, possibly leaving a set of trebles in the pike's throat. If in doubt, replace it with a new one. The cost of 20 in of wire to those who make their own traces is not worth thinking about (see 'Trace making' p. 44).

LEDGERED LIVEBAIT RIGS

Although livebaits usually work best when presented beneath floats and simultaneously provide immense visual enjoyment, there are situations which demand a ledgered bait because floats are impractical: for presenting the bait to pike on the bottom of deep, swirling weir pools, for instance, or pike occupying deep gullies far out in lakes or gravel pits, or during gale force conditions when any sort of float fishing is impossible.

Make up a simple running ledger as in fig. 19 with a

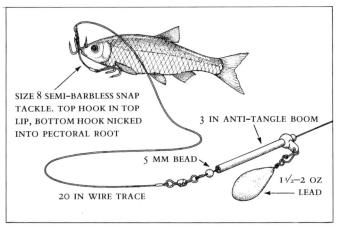

FIGURE 19 *Ledgered*
livebait rigs

1–2 oz bomb clipped on to a 3 in anti-tangle boom stopped with a bead against the swivel of the 20 in snap-tackle trace. This gives an effective rig that casts well and presents the bait close to the bottom. To present the bait well off bottom to pike working the upper water layers, or to avoid the bait tangling with dense bottom weeds or snags, consider the benefits of the sunken float rig in fig. 20. Again the set-up is kept simple, and is rather like the bottom end of the running float paternoster. Use a long bomb link with a Drennan clear plastic subfloat running free on the line. This rises and supports the livebait at the desired depth once the line has been tightened from reel to rig.

For bite indication when using these rigs, the drop-arm indicator is recommended because tension can be applied at the line clip to allow for constant pulling from the bait (see p. 52).

DEADBAITING

Until the 1950s, specifically setting out to catch pike using deadbaits, particularly static deadbaits, was a technique practised by very few. It would even have been considered rather eccentric. Small dead fish – fresh, preserved or pickled – were mounted on spinning flights and spun or 'wobbled', to use the term by which we now present moving deadbaits. However, to hope for a pike to suck up

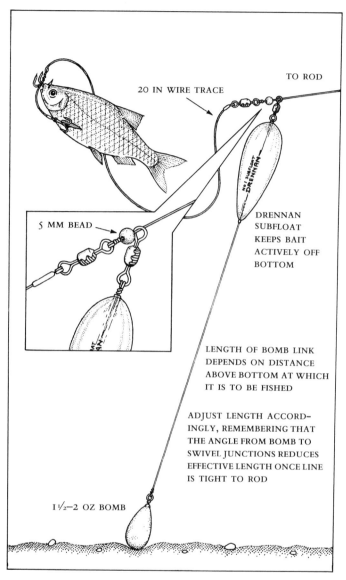

FIGURE 20 *Ledgered livebait rigs*

TO ROD

20 IN WIRE TRACE

5 MM BEAD

DRENNAN
SUBFLOAT
KEEPS BAIT
ACTIVELY OFF
BOTTOM

LENGTH OF BOMB LINK
DEPENDS ON DISTANCE
ABOVE BOTTOM AT WHICH
IT IS TO BE FISHED

ADJUST LENGTH ACCORD-
INGLY, REMEMBERING THAT
THE ANGLE FROM BOMB TO
SWIVEL JUNCTIONS REDUCES
EFFECTIVE LENGTH ONCE LINE
IS TIGHT TO ROD

1½–2 OZ BOMB

a deadbait lying completely static on the bottom would have seemed an impractical method to the majority of pike anglers just 40 years ago. This must seem strange to the young pike fishermen of today, because most tackle shops carry a huge range of freshly frozen, coloured and natural deadbaits. Even during the harshest winter weather (when catching livebaits would be next to impossible), provided the surface is not iced over we can set out for a day's pike fishing with fresh baits readily available. Thus has life changed, and in many ways so have our attitudes towards pike fishing and pike baits. I mentioned earlier the devastating pressure that can be put on small shoal fish and small fisheries by over-culling them to obtain livebaits, a fact that most pike fishermen are now fully aware of. Many take a responsible attitude by using sea, or estuary deadbaits, rainbow trout or eels, the culling of which does not affect indigenous freshwater stocks.

Besides, it is a fact that big, fat old female pike in the majority of waters are far more susceptible to sucking up a static deadbait from the bottom than they are to chasing about after livebaits, particularly in heavily coloured waters where the pike's senses are geared decidedly more towards smelling out their food than sighting and chasing it. And so, presenting the easily located and taken 'static' deadbait has become the big-fish method in the majority of fisheries; except, perhaps, those clear-flowing rivers where the pike invariably show a preference for a moving bait.

THE STATIC DEADBAIT

Float fishing stillwaters

The most enjoyable and effective way of presenting the static deadbait is beneath a float, because apart from minimizing resistance to a pike taking the bait (compared, say, to ledgering with a heavy bomb) a float also gives you something nice to watch. There really is nothing quite like observing the drunken antics of a deadbait float. It is almost possible to imagine what is going on down below by relating it to the movements of the float. There is of course no set pattern. Initially the float may twitch, bob or jerk a few times as the pike sucks up the bait and turns it for swallowing, then slowly move away and beneath the surface, the line tightening as it goes. Or with absolutely no prior indication whatsoever, the float may suddenly disappear and the line zing tight as the pike moves confidently away. In this case, either the initial bob or twitch of the float was so slight it was not noticed, or the pike sucked up the bait and swallowed it all in one gulp, as they do, and moved off immediately.

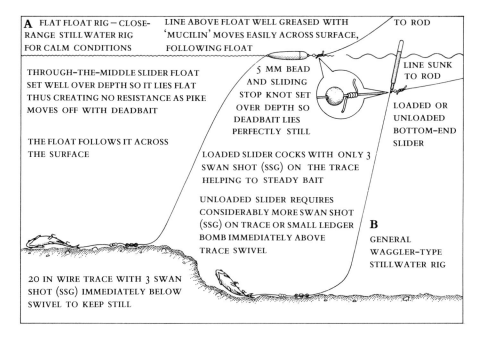

A FLAT FLOAT RIG – CLOSE-RANGE STILL WATER RIG FOR CALM CONDITIONS

LINE ABOVE FLOAT WELL GREASED WITH 'MUCILIN' MOVES EASILY ACROSS SURFACE, FOLLOWING FLOAT

TO ROD

THROUGH-THE-MIDDLE SLIDER FLOAT SET WELL OVER DEPTH SO IT LIES FLAT THUS CREATING NO RESISTANCE AS PIKE MOVES OFF WITH DEADBAIT

5 MM BEAD AND SLIDING STOP KNOT SET OVER DEPTH SO DEADBAIT LIES PERFECTLY STILL

LINE SUNK TO ROD

LOADED OR UNLOADED BOTTOM-END SLIDER

THE FLOAT FOLLOWS IT ACROSS THE SURFACE

LOADED SLIDER COCKS WITH ONLY 3 SWAN SHOT (SSG) ON THE TRACE HELPING TO STEADY BAIT

UNLOADED SLIDER REQUIRES CONSIDERABLY MORE SWAN SHOT (SSG) ON TRACE OR SMALL LEDGER BOMB IMMEDIATELY ABOVE TRACE SWIVEL

B GENERAL WAGGLER-TYPE STILLWATER RIG

20 IN WIRE TRACE WITH 3 SWAN SHOT (SSG) IMMEDIATELY BELOW SWIVEL TO KEEP STILL

I prefer a sliding float with the line (greased above the float) passing through the centre for close-range work in stillwaters, where it won't get blown about and thus move the bait, as in the flat float rig (fig. 21A). For general fishing and most other situations, including really windy weather, consider the waggler-type rig in fig. 21B, where the line passes through the bottom eye and is sunk from float to rod tip just as in waggler fishing for other species in stillwaters.

FIGURE 21 *The float-fished static deadbait in stillwaters*

The secret of presenting a deadbait beneath a float lies in ensuring that it remains absolutely static. Pike will then confidently suck it up, but not if the float is set too shallow causing the bait's tail to be monotonously lifted up each time the float bobs up and down with the waves. You would not expect a bream, for instance, to readily accept bread flake presented on a waggler rig set too shallow, causing the bait to drag unnaturally along the bottom in stillwater; and a pike will show the same degree of natural caution. I was almost tempted to say intelligence because at times pike do show a remarkable degree of sensitivity. This is why I like to set the sliding float well over depth, whether it fishes flat or upright; at least twice as deep as the swim, so that at least a couple of feet of line lie along the bottom in addition to the trace and bait. In no way will the

pike then feel any degree of buoyancy from the float as it
engulfs the bait in its jaws. And as a result you will
experience very few dropped runs using static deadbaits.

Running water rigs

In really slow-moving rivers use the general waggler rig in
fig. 22 with a small bomb on the line above the trace to
ensure the bait lies static. But for fast-running water,
because it lies flat and cannot be submerged by the flow,
the close-range flat float rig (fig. 16, p. 83) is ideal so long
as the cast is made directly downstream and the rod tip
angled upwards to keep the line off the surface. Those who
like to stret peg for roach or chub during the winter
months will know all about the mechanics of presenting a
static bait with this method.

With both of these float rigs, after tightening up and
positioning the rod on two rests set horizontally, the bale
arm is opened and a loop of line clipped beneath an elastic
band or run clip fixed around the handle. This is a safety

FIGURE 22 *Flat float
ledger rig for fast-
running water*

measure against the occasional suicidal pike that really belts
off with the bait, and of course against those unforgivable

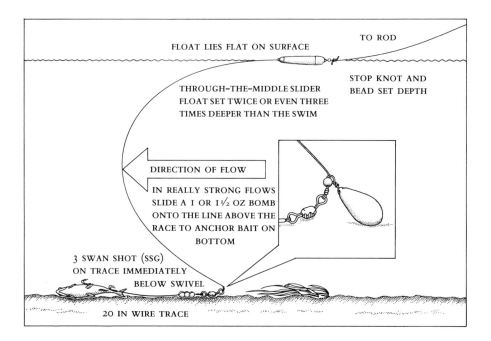

FLOAT LIES FLAT ON SURFACE

TO ROD

THROUGH–THE–MIDDLE SLIDER
FLOAT SET TWICE OR EVEN THREE
TIMES DEEPER THAN THE SWIM

STOP KNOT AND
BEAD SET DEPTH

DIRECTION OF FLOW

IN REALLY STRONG FLOWS
SLIDE A 1 OR 1½ OZ BOMB
ONTO THE LINE ABOVE THE
RACE TO ANCHOR BAIT ON
BOTTOM

3 SWAN SHOT (SSG)
ON TRACE IMMEDIATELY
BELOW SWIVEL

20 IN WIRE TRACE

occasions when you failed to notice the float trundling away. We are all human, and there is no point in losing a rod and reel from the rests through sloppiness.

As when livebaiting, I prefer to strike straight away when presenting static deadbaits, on the basis that if it comes off it was probably a small pike anyway.

Half baits

I only ever use relatively small whole baits, say up to 7–8 in long – smelt, herrings and the like. In fact, for most static deadbait situations these days I much prefer to use half baits. I am certain that when cut in half the freshness and oily attractiveness of a deadbait permeates considerably quicker through stillwater, and of course even the size of a

No wonder Bruce Vaughan looks ecstatic. He hit the jackpot with this still-water 24-pounder. It sucked up an air-injected deadbait suspended just off the bottom in 14 ft of water.

half mackerel is nothing compared to the size of the jaws of a 10 lb pike. With enhanced attraction and increased hooking potential, the half bait has much to offer on the strike when you heave the rod back into a powerful curve. In addition, and this is a very valid point, with very lightly hooked pike thrashing on the surface prior to netting, being that much lighter half baits do not act like a disgorger anywhere near as much as whole baits.

FIGURE 23 *Mount-ing half baits*

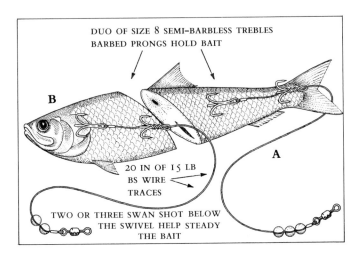

DUO OF SIZE 8 SEMI–BARBLESS TREBLES
BARBED PRONGS HOLD BAIT

B

A

20 IN OF 15 LB
BS WIRE
TRACES

TWO OR THREE SWAN SHOT BELOW
THE SWIVEL HELP STEADY
THE BAIT

The best way of presentation is to cut the bait in half diagonally and mount it as in fig. 23, using the standard duo (snap-tackle) of semi-barbless size 8 trebles. Using larger trebles is not necessary regardless of the pike's size. Size 8s provide a good purchase in both bait and pike while allowing the bait to be sucked in easily without suspicion. Note how in fig. 23B the head end is mounted, on the assumption that the pike will recognize the shape and swallow it head first. Thus the trebles will be pointing the correct way for striking, although I admit this does not always happen. Sometimes the bait is even swallowed tail first, but it is wise to assume that pike swallow fish head first so they go down easily, whereas the tail might stick across the throat opening.

I know that many pike anglers hesitate about using the head end of a deadbait, and actually throw them away, which is a great pity. I have yet to experience pike refusing heads and if anything, with that eye shining up, they look more like the real thing than the favoured tail end.

Whole baits

When offering whole baits, fix the duo of trebles firmly into the tail root and along the flank as in fig. 24, with a distance of around 3 in between hooks. This allows the pike to swallow a good half of the bait before the hooks enter the throat tissue, and will result in few deeply hooked pike.

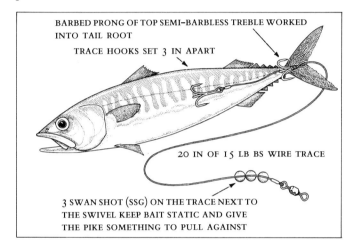

BARBED PRONG OF TOP SEMI-BARBLESS TREBLE WORKED INTO TAIL ROOT

TRACE HOOKS SET 3 IN APART

20 IN OF 15 LB BS WIRE TRACE

3 SWAN SHOT (SSG) ON THE TRACE NEXT TO THE SWIVEL KEEP BAIT STATIC AND GIVE THE PIKE SOMETHING TO PULL AGAINST

FIGURE 24 *Presenting a whole, static deadbait*

Pike do occasionally (after being caught on them several times) become suspicious of the static deadbait always lying flat on the bottom, and to buoy its head upwards by injecting it with air or inserting foam strip can produce

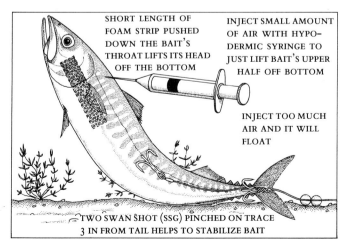

SHORT LENGTH OF FOAM STRIP PUSHED DOWN THE BAIT'S THROAT LIFTS ITS HEAD OFF THE BOTTOM

INJECT SMALL AMOUNT OF AIR WITH HYPO-DERMIC SYRINGE TO JUST LIFT BAIT'S UPPER HALF OFF BOTTOM

INJECT TOO MUCH AIR AND IT WILL FLOAT

TWO SWAN SHOT (SSG) PINCHED ON TRACE 3 IN FROM TAIL HELPS TO STABILIZE BAIT

FIGURE 25 *Presenting a whole static deadbait*

runs from spooky fish (see fig. 25). Pinch two or three swan shot on the trace just 3 in from the bait's tail to keep its lower half on the bottom.

You will notice three swan shot on the trace next to the swivel in fig. 24. These help to steady the bait and provide a little 'something' for the pike to pull against (without creating enough resistance to make it drop the bait). It then moves away from the direction of the rod and thus registers a positive as opposed to a slack line run.

FREELINING AND LEDGERING

When weather conditions, especially high winds, render float fishing impossible, or the deadbait needs to be cast long distances at which the float is impractical, say 50 yds plus, then a simple freeline or ledger rig is used.

I dislike using any appreciable amount of weight on the line (apart from three swan shot on the trace) when presenting static deadbaits, unless absolutely necessary. Heavy bombs lessen the sensitivity of the static bait, and because the line passes through while the bomb stays put (often creating a right angle of line between bait and rod tip) striking also could be impaired (see fig. 26A). Whereas with a freelined bait the line simply follows the route of the pike and is easy to straighten for a quick, positive strike (see fig. 26B).

FIGURE 26 *The effectiveness of a simple freelined static deadbait*

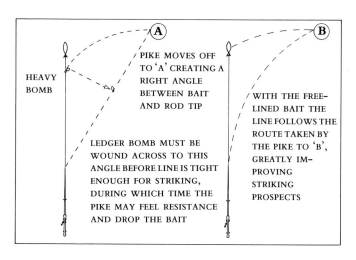

A
PIKE MOVES OFF TO 'A' CREATING A RIGHT ANGLE BETWEEN BAIT AND ROD TIP

HEAVY BOMB

LEDGER BOMB MUST BE WOUND ACROSS TO THIS ANGLE BEFORE LINE IS TIGHT ENOUGH FOR STRIKING, DURING WHICH TIME THE PIKE MAY FEEL RESISTANCE AND DROP THE BAIT

B
WITH THE FREE-LINED BAIT THE LINE FOLLOWS THE ROUTE TAKEN BY THE PIKE TO 'B', GREATLY IM-PROVING STRIKING PROSPECTS

Provided the bait (with just three, or a maximum of four swan shot on the trace) can be cast to the desired spot (and a mackerel tail can easily be pushed 60 yd out), a freelined bait is best. If not, then rig up a simple ledger with the bomb attached to a 4 in anti-tangle boom sliding above the

Irish pike are renowned for putting a healthy bend in your rod. A nice fish hooked at distance on a ledgered deadbait is netted for Terry Smith by Hugh Gough, angling officer of the Central Fisheries Board.

Using electric bite alarms in conjunction with drop-arm indicators, Simon Earp from Norwich mounts a fresh deadbait to be presented way out into a deep trough in a Norfolk gravel pit.

trace (as in fig. 27). Remember to use a bead as a cushion between boom and trace swivel. As there will now be two points of weight flying through the air (bomb and bait), distance and accuracy will be improved if the bait size is kept to a minimum. Small, firm-bodied whole fish of between 4 and 5 in cast well.

FIGURE 27 *Simple, distance static deadbait rig*

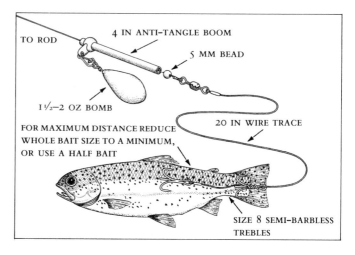

Whether freelining or ledgering the static deadbait, bites are best registered on drop-off/arm indicators, which fit on the rear rod rests and clip to the line once the bale arm has been opened (see p. 52). As a precaution against deeply hooked pike, strike any indication of a bite immediately when ledgering or freelining.

Ledgering, again using the drop arm as bite indicator, is an effective way of presenting the static deadbait in running water. To minimize water pressure against the line, set the rod on two rests with the tip angled up high. Very often a definite 'knock' is seen on the rod tip (just as when ledgering for chub) as the pike sucks the bait up before moving off, at which point the line should be released from the indicator and the rod held. There then comes an eerie sensation as the line slips positively through the fingers in response to the run of the pike. But don't let it run too far. Close the bale arm and as soon as the fish's weight plus the current pulls the rod over into a full bend, whack the hooks home hard. To effectively subdue a really big pike hooked in fast currents, quickly try to get below the fish so it has both current and your rod tip to fight.

FISHING AT NIGHT

Presenting static deadbaits during darkness is something worth trying on clear-watered rivers, lakes or pits which receive regular attention from daytime pike fishermen.

Pike are certainly no different to all other species in that they become far less suspicious of baits offered them under the cloak of darkness. I must admit that setting off in the dark to fish for pike after a day's work on a cold and frosty evening is not exactly my idea of fun. I suppose this is common with many anglers, because I think nothing of freezing my toes off for several dark hours watching an illuminated quiver tip in search of big roach or chub.

A friend who specializes in this field and has done for several years, Nick Beardmore, hedges his bets when night pike fishing his local River Bure by pre-baiting for over a week prior to actually fishing. He also chooses a comfortable night and favourable weather pattern as opposed to a raging gale or a rapidly falling thermometer.

The pre-baiting consists of introducing a dozen deadbaits cut into halves (small fish like sprats are left whole) scattered over two separate areas or swims, quite close into the bank. These are introduced as darkness falls to coincide with the moment when he intends to start fishing, and to eradicate attention from waterbirds. Cormorants and grebes are common throughout the Bure as they are in most fisheries, and there is no point whatsoever in tempting providence.

Although the tidal River Bure, with its network of connecting boatyards, dykes and large broads, contains massive numbers of pike, they become very wary as a result of over-fishing. Matters naturally improve for a while after heavy rain, when the river colours up, but once it clears again, daytime sport deteriorates. So fishing at night is a natural progression.

The point of pre-baiting two separate areas is that should the first fail to produce for any reason, after an hour you can move and try the next. In fact, if fishing at night starts to catch on, there is nothing to stop you pre-baiting and keeping several swims going.

Take along just two rods and start by placing one bait really close into the bank, with the second further out or

Spooky pike living in hard-fished, clear-water fisheries respond to static deadbaits with far more enthusiasm at night, as Bruce Vaughan knows only too well.

deliberately next to a particular feature. Use simple freeline tactics with two or three swan shot on the trace next to the swivel, adding a bomb above the trace only to counteract a strong flow when river fishing.

For bite indication use drop arms or monkey climbers which incorporate luminous betalight elements, or simply illuminate the indicators with a wide-beam, low-powered torch laid on the ground away from the water and your line of vision.

WOBBLING

Retrieving a small dead fish mounted head first on the trace so that pike assume it is alive and grab hold, is an extremely effective and exciting technique guaranteed to keep you casting and thinking all day long, just as in lure fishing.

It is also a very versatile, mobile method which provides total coverage of any given area. For instance, if you like to fish with a two-rod set-up to increase your chances in big

Using a wobbled deadbait in a grid searching pattern provides total coverage of large stillwaters. This angler is not afraid to play her pike hard to make them tail-walk.

stillwaters, but nothing is coming to the static deadbaits being presented on each, reel one in and cover the area in more depth by wobbling a deadbait in a grid-searching pattern. A total blank when pike are not moving around and hunting out your static baits, can be turned into an exciting session by taking the bait to the fish through continually searching with a wobbled bait. This situation occurs most commonly in deep, coloured lakes and pits during long periods of low light values, such as day upon day of overcast weather. Unless you almost hit a pike on the head with a wobbled deadbait they simply do not move about much. The situation can, of course, change instantly if the weather does, when the strong rays of the sun penetrate deep, dark water. Suddenly pike are on the move, and in a short feeding burst several runs might come to previously untouched static deadbaits in as many minutes. Such feeding sprees, however, rarely last more than a couple of hours, and a switch to working the wobbled deadbait (still leaving one static on the bottom) could well keep pike coming to the net throughout the rest of the day.

To mount deadbaits for wobbling, fix the trebles so they are just 3 in apart by wrapping the wire around the shank of the upper treble, and firmly embed two of its prongs into the bait's eye socket. The bottom treble is nicked with the barbed prong only into the bait's flank along the lateral line (see fig. 28). The deadbait is now firmly rigged for casting and when retrieved will wobble attractively. When the top hook eventually pulls through the socket, re-rig on the other side.

FIGURE 28 Hooking a deadbait for wobbling

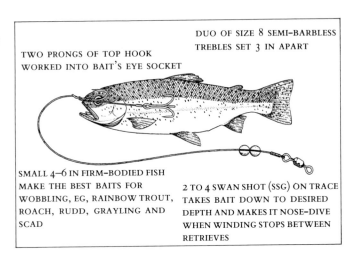

DUO OF SIZE 8 SEMI-BARBLESS TREBLES SET 3 IN APART

TWO PRONGS OF TOP HOOK WORKED INTO BAIT'S EYE SOCKET

SMALL 4–6 IN FIRM-BODIED FISH MAKE THE BEST BAITS FOR WOBBLING, EG, RAINBOW TROUT, ROACH, RUDD, GRAYLING AND SCAD

2 TO 4 SWAN SHOT (SSG) ON TRACE TAKES BAIT DOWN TO DESIRED DEPTH AND MAKES IT NOSE-DIVE WHEN WINDING STOPS BETWEEN RETRIEVES

For fishing over thick weed or in shallow water do not add any weight to the trace, but to keep the bait down close to the bottom where pike lie during the colder months you will need somewhere between two and four swan shot pinched on to the trace immediately below the swivel. It all depends on the depth and the rate at which you retrieve.

Where the bottom contours vary due to weed-beds, shallow bars, snags and so on, you need to retrieve the bait well up lest it catches, say, 3 or 4 ft above where you imagine the bottom to be. In lakes and pits of even depth where the bottom is clear, however, you can twitch the bait along, almost bumping pike on the nose. To do this, allow the bait to reach bottom before starting the retrieve. Then wind erratically, but very slowly; try to 'feel' what is happening down below. Keep the rod tip at an angle to the bait and watch it for any indication of a taking fish. Every so often give the tip a jerk or a twitch, followed by a couple of fast turns on the reel handle. Then pause, allowing the bait to nose-dive for a couple of feet before twitching it back up again (as in fig. 29). Remember that the swan shots hit bottom ahead of the bait, so if you lift it quickly upwards you will not pick up much bottom debris. In the past this technique was called sink and draw because you allowed the bait to sink before drawing it up again.

Now for the strike. Do not wait for the pike to grab and

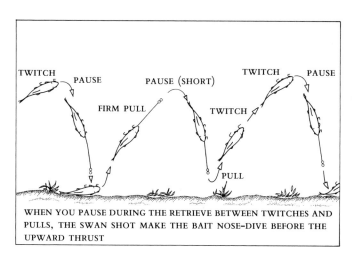

FIGURE 29 *Make your wobbled deadbait come to life on the retrieve by pulling and jerking it erratically.*

TWITCH
PAUSE
PAUSE (SHORT)
TWITCH
PAUSE
FIRM PULL
TWITCH
TWITCH
PULL

WHEN YOU PAUSE DURING THE RETRIEVE BETWEEN TWITCHES AND PULLS, THE SWAN SHOT MAKE THE BAIT NOSE-DIVE BEFORE THE UPWARD THRUST

then turn the bait in its jaws by giving it free line when you feel a 'take'. Pike react completely differently when snatching at a wobbled deadbait from when sucking up a resistance-free static from the bottom, when time is given. So unless you want the pike to drop the bait, whack it immediately by winding quickly down until you feel its full weight, and follow through with a long, powerful strike to put the hooks home, striking a second time to make doubly sure. At this point the pike tries to eject the bait by opening its jaws and shaking its head, so keep a good bend in the rod or the hooks will drop out. Point the rod directly at the pike while quickly winding down to it prior to striking to minimize slack and elasticity in the line.

*John's brother,
David, wobbles for
pike immediately
below a weir on Hert-
fordshire's River Lee,
using a paternoster
bomb link to keep the
bait just above bottom
in the deep swirling
waters.*

Wobbling in running water

In slow-moving water, mounting and retrieving the
wobbled deadbait is exactly the same as in stillwater and it
is great fun to work the bait purposefully alongside regular
pike hideouts such as overhanging or sunken willows and
have it taken at the very place you imagined a pike to be
lying. This is reading the water at its very best, and
provides a mobile method of fishing where, with a
pocketful of fresh baits, miles of winding river can be
searched, wobbling beside all the 'feature' swims.

In deep, cold, fast rivers, however, where pike keep
close to the bottom, a slightly different approach is called
for, in the form of a 3 ft nylon kink joined to the reel line
1 ft above the trace (see fig. 30). A small bomb goes on the
business end for bouncing along the bottom. A snap
swivel allows for a quick change of bombs.

This rig ensures that the bait works just above the pike's
immediate field of vision, which is so important, especially
in coloured water. Bumping the bait systematically across
the bottom of a deep weir pool, for instance, can be great
fun, resulting in some thunderous takes, and apart from
ledgering the bait, no other method ensures the bait is
actively presented just off bottom where the vast majority
of cold-water pike will be lying.

As when wobbling in the usual manner, strike the
minute the pike grabs hold, with a long, hard, sweeping
strike, taking a step or two backwards to keep that rod

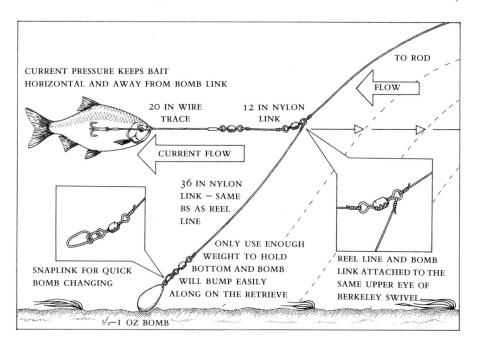

CURRENT PRESSURE KEEPS BAIT
HORIZONTAL AND AWAY FROM BOMB LINK

TO ROD

FLOW

20 IN WIRE   12 IN NYLON
   TRACE   LINK

CURRENT FLOW

36 IN NYLON
LINK – SAME
BS AS REEL
LINE

ONLY USE ENOUGH
WEIGHT TO HOLD
BOTTOM AND BOMB
WILL BUMP EASILY
ALONG ON THE RETRIEVE

SNAPLINK FOR QUICK
BOMB CHANGING

REEL LINE AND BOMB
LINK ATTACHED TO THE
SAME UPPER EYE OF
BERKELEY SWIVEL

½–1 OZ BOMB

fully bent, lest the fish manages some slack and ejects the
bait.

FIGURE 30 *Wobbling in running water*

FLOAT-DRIFTING DEADBAITS

Float-drifting deadbaits is a method which really works
best and covers the maximum area from an anchored boat
(see 'Boat fishing' p. 123), but may be used to good effect
in large stillwaters fished from a headland when there is a
strong wind coming from behind (see fig. 31). The line
must be greased so that it floats well. Note how, by
allowing a belly to form between rod tip and float, the
same line can be held as the rig is taken down the lake (line
must be given during this time from an open spool) until it
comes to rest in the lee of the wind, having covered and
possibly shown the bait to pike lying over an enormous
area. Start by casting a short way out, and once the bait
comes to rest downwind retrieve slowly (in case a pike
takes the bait on the way in), then recast a little further out
each time. Using the wind and waves to bounce the bait
attractively about is a fascinating way of presenting a
deadbait to pike, which in many cases assume the bait to be
live due to its erratic action.

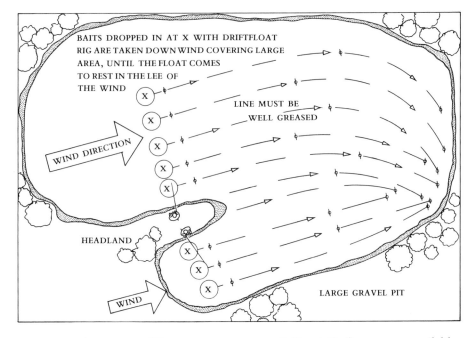

BAITS DROPPED IN AT X WITH DRIFTFLOAT
RIG ARE TAKEN DOWN WIND COVERING LARGE
AREA, UNTIL THE FLOAT COMES
TO REST IN THE LEE OF
THE WIND

LINE MUST BE
WELL GREASED

WIND DIRECTION

HEADLAND

WIND

LARGE GRAVEL PIT

FIGURE 31 *Float-drifting deadbaits or livebaits*

There are numerous sail-like drift floats now available, like the original ET Drifter shown in fig. 32. Note how the bait is presented horizontally to simulate the position of a live fish. It can be set to fish at any depth from within 2 ft of the bottom upwards, and in coloured water it is best presented closer to the bottom. In reality, however, taking into account a large area of water where, during the drift on a particular line or arc, depths of 10 to 18 ft of water may be encountered, my advice would be to set the float (easily rigged as a slider with bead and stop knot above) to fish the deadbait at 9 ft. It will then not foul bottom and has the possibility of attracting pike from almost every depth if the water is not too coloured. The beauty of drift-fishing is that as so much water is covered, action can come at any time from the moment when the bait is first plopped in to over 100 yd away. It is imperative when drift fishing to use a long, powerful rod and have the spool of your reel full to the brim with fresh line, otherwise distance will definitely be limited.

The best way of rigging the ET Drifter is with the line passing through the small, detachable ring on top of the stem and then through the swivel at the bottom of the stem, so the greased line floats easily on the surface throughout the drift. A sharp pull at the end of the drift, or

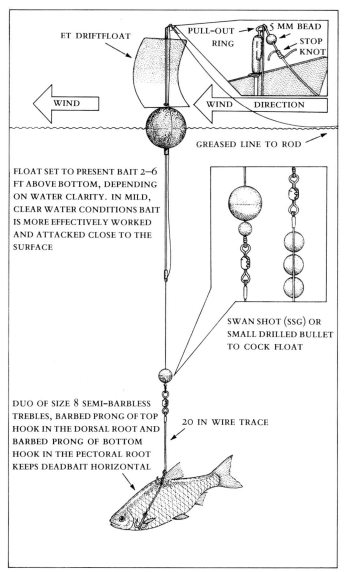

FIGURE 32 *Driftfloat rig*

ET DRIFTFLOAT

PULL-OUT RING

5 MM BEAD
STOP KNOT

WIND

WIND DIRECTION

GREASED LINE TO ROD

FLOAT SET TO PRESENT BAIT 2–6 FT ABOVE BOTTOM, DEPENDING ON WATER CLARITY. IN MILD, CLEAR WATER CONDITIONS BAIT IS MORE EFFECTIVELY WORKED AND ATTACKED CLOSE TO THE SURFACE

SWAN SHOT (SSG) OR SMALL DRILLED BULLET TO COCK FLOAT

DUO OF SIZE 8 SEMI-BARBLESS TREBLES, BARBED PRONG OF TOP HOOK IN THE DORSAL ROOT AND BARBED PRONG OF BOTTOM HOOK IN THE PECTORAL ROOT KEEPS DEADBAIT HORIZONTAL

20 IN WIRE TRACE

indeed when a run occurs and the pike is struck, will release the line from the top ring, instantly converting the drifter to a waggler (bottom end only) for easy retrieval.

Drifting livebaits

The only difference is in swapping the deadbait for a small livebait. Remember to fix the hooks as described in the livebaiting section (p. 60), with one barbed prong of the top treble through the bait's top lip and one prong of the bottom treble nicked into its pectoral root – semi-barbless size 8s, of course.

Striking

So long as the clutch is adjusted correctly there is little chance of the line being taken beyond its point of elasticity, even at close range. John gives a big double-figure pike some stick while boat-fishing a lake in southern Ireland.

When the float suddenly sinks to a pike which has grabbed the bait (alive or dead) 80 to over 100 yd away, it is not enough simply to wind down until the line is tight, and then strike. The amount of stretch in even 50 yd of 10 lb monofilament is enormous, and when contemplating setting the hooks successfully with twice as much line out, a new approach is required. In fact, there is no way of striking the hooks home when distance fishing. You simply point the rod at the pike, tighten up the clutch on your reel (so it does not slip under pressure and cause line twist) and keep winding like a person possessed until you feel the weight of the fish. And you keep on winding, and dragging the pike towards you, until it senses danger and opens its jaws to eject the bait. At this point, so long as the

line is kept tight, the hooks should catch hold. A really big fish just may swim off in the opposite direction and help to pull the hooks home, but most pike will be led towards the rod for quite some distance. Once the pike's head-shaking routine has been transmitted up the line and the hooks are obviously well in, readjust the reel's clutch, keep the rod in a full curve and enjoy the fight.

ARTIFICIAL LURE FISHING

I say this quite without reservation: if you can catch pike regularly from a wide spectrum of waters by fooling them into munching artificial lures constructed from quite alien materials such as plastic, copper, aluminium, steel, brass or wood, then by comparison every other technique should prove delightfully easy.

When working artificials, the rod should be pointed at the lure throughout the retrieve. The line is then protected from snapping by the elasticity in standard monofilament. Do not use low-stretch brands.

Without question, catching regularly on lures demands an optimum level of skill, and you need to have a fair idea of each fisheries character: the depths, the snags (otherwise it is costly for obvious reasons), the visible and non-visible

sub-surface habitats preferred by pike and so on. In other words, by pulling lures you enjoy a complete involvement with your quarry.

Unfortunately, far too many pike anglers only ever pull a lure when other techniques fail. They wait until sport is non-existant on deadbaits or livebaits, or both, and then give the rusty spinner in the bottom of their tackle box a few casts at a time when conditions are unfavourable whatever the method. Naturally, their preconceived idea that lures only occasionally produce the goods are substantiated, and so they contentedly return to watching stationary indicators, or floats which are not going to disappear. Were they to think a little harder, however, and reason that perhaps it just might be a poor day, and that whatever the method pike are going to be unco-operative (even then I would still rate lures the best bet due to the sheer amount of water that can be covered in a day), the session could at least be put to good use by clipping on a heavy spoon and plummeting the depths all around the lake or pit for future occasions. By leaving the bale arm open after casting and using the countdown method (applicable to any sinking lure) of allowing roughly one foot in descent for every second counted, it is a simple and most enjoyable way of plummeting to obtain an accurate idea of the depth, plus the exact whereabouts of shallow bars, plateaux, holes, gullies and so on. I favour heavy spoons for this wandering technique because they can be cast long distances, and flutter down to the bottom in an attractive way. Pike have grabbed hold so many times after just one turn of the handle to lift the spoon from the bottom at the start of the retrieve, that it cannot be coincidence.

Pike hear the spoon's arrival on the surface, and in clear water visually follow its route all the way down to the bottom, as they do with sinking lures. Some advice is in order at this point on how the rod should be held when retrieving artificial lures, including spoons, because if you get it wrong, a large number of pike will manage to slip the hooks and get away. Throughout the retrieve hold the rod with the tip pointing at the lure, with just the slightest sideways deviation for twitching and jerking. If you hold the rod to one side, the hooks may not be driven home on the strike because of the incredible amount of stretch in monofilament. There is no chance of the line snapping with the rod pointing directly at the pike. Besides, when the hooks are felt to bite, you can raise the rod into its full curve and rely on the pre-set clutch to give line whenever the pike runs.

Occasionally, and this is more noticeable when you are fishing on a short line, pike will hit the artificial really hard and belt off all in one lovely, arm-wrenching movement, banging the hooks in hard as they turn. To facilitate hooking I doctor the trebles on most lures by gently flattening all the barbs down, then hone each prong to a needlepoint with a file. This indispensible item I keep in the back pocket of my waist-coat so it is always at the ready. Lure trebles soon blunt from being continually retrieved through thick weeds, hitting the bottom and, of course, biting into the bone of a pike's jaw. And for the price of a good-quality file (which costs little more than just one lure), to fish with anything less than really sharp hooks is foolhardy.

As mentioned in the trace-making section (see p. 44), for all lure fishing I prefer a wire trace of around 10 in long, with a plain swivel at one end to which the reel line is tied, and a Berkely cross-lok at the other for speedy lure changing. Over-long traces tend to kink rather easily, but even with a short one be prepared to inspect it regularly for signs of wear, changing it immediately if in the slightest doubt. Continual casting puts tremendous strain on the last few yards of line and eventually takes it beyond the point of elasticity, especially the piece between trace and bale arm. So don't wait for a sudden snap-off to occur on the cast sending the lure out all by itself, periodically (twice a day if you are enjoying a long session) remove this last section and retie the lure.

I make no apologies for digressing at this point to mention what to some may be a host of minor details, because when added together the impact can make all the difference to whether you regularly catch and learn to fish with confidence using artificial lures – or never come to grips with what is undoubtedly the most fascinating of techniques.

As I mentioned previously, using a spoon is just one way of depth finding; an echo-sounder is the most effective but costly method (see p. 57). If you already fish a particular pike water for other species, you will no doubt

*Artificial lures work
really well in clear
water. Retrieve in
erratic movements,
anticipating that a
pike might be follow-
ing and could be
induced to grab hold
by any sudden
'crippled' action im-
parted by the rod tip.*

already have a reasonable idea of its topography. The point
is that many artificial lures have been designed not only to
wiggle or dive or vibrate in a particular way due to their
shape or weight, but to work in a particular depth band.

Take plugs, for instance, which fall into three basic
categories: floaters, floating divers and sinking divers. It is
pointless working a floating surface popper across 14 ft of
cold water. In no way will the pike lying on the bottom
shoot up and grab hold. By the same token, a sinking diver
tossed into dense lily-pads, where it will become immobile
after one crank of the reel handle, is equally useless. You
really need to know the capabilities of each and every
artificial in your lure box, whether it floats, sinks or dives,
and the respective depths to which each will dive on the
retrieve; and, of course, their action (see pp. 76–80).

It is then a case of selecting a suitable artificial for the
type of water or habitat at hand and making it come alive.
For instance, and this applies particularly to clear water
conditions, when a pike is following but will not hit,
suddenly start speeding up the retrieve, making it faster
and faster until you completely run out of water. It may
well seem that time has run out, but then right at the last
second the pike will make a lunge and grab hold with
unbelievable speed. Do not chicken out and slow up over
the last few yards or the pike will do the same and swim off
disgruntled.

Conversely, when working lures deep down in coloured

water the retrieve needs to be slow in order to allow the pike time to home in on it and grab hold. One particular session comes to mind which perfectly illustrates this. I was boat-fishing a large, deep lake near Norwich with an old friend, Bruce Vaughan, from Oxford, and following several days of strong winds the usually clear water became heavily coloured in a brown peaty hue, providing less than 18 in of visibility.

We had in fact accounted for several nice fish to 18 lb on static deadbaits during the morning with nothing on lures. In the later afternoon, we spotted through binoculars a huge concentration of fry near the surface, just out from a thick reed promontory over on the opposite side of the 20 acre lake, obviously with pike in attendance (fry could be seen regularly scattering on the surface). We upped anchor and immediately moved position to cover the area.

Big spoons and floating/diving plugs worked through the upper water layers where the occasional pike could be seen lunging through the fry, produced not a single follow. But as soon as I swapped lures to a spinner bait, which can be retrieved slower than just about all other sub-surface artificials, pike started hitting. After taking several pike various spoons were tried again but with not the slightest interest, yet here was a situation with dozens and dozens of pike gorging themselves on fry. As we unhooked them, young roach and bream in the 1–2 in class were spewed up by the dozen, some still alive.

As soon as a spinner bait was clipped back on to the trace and retrieved through the fry shoals, pike were on it straight away. To cut a very long story short, because in a hectic three-hour spell Bruce and I must have accounted for at least 20 pike ranging from 6 lb up to 17 lb, we repeatedly switched back and forth from spinner baits to other lures, with every single pike falling to the slow retrieval of the spinner bait. It was uncanny, and exactly the kind of phenomenon you believe cannot possibly occur until it happens to you.

It certainly brought home to me the importance of a slow retrieval when the water is heavily coloured. Of course, in crystal-clear water it is often possible to watch the reactions of pike in pursuit of the artificial, and by winding erratically, jerking, twitching, and using the rod tip to create movement, irritate it into attacking. There are many occasions when pike grab an artificial through nothing but sheer frustration; after all, small fish never behave like artificial lures.

Summer plugging

Working artificials through lily-pads alongside sedge beds or between narrow channels in dense reed-beds to bring pike out for an attack also calls for a slow retrieve. Indeed, putting live, crippled action into surface plugs and weedless lures is arguably the most thrilling and explosive method of catching pike. It creates suspense because you never really know from the moment the lure hits the water when the take is going to come. There could be a violent, sudden eruption as the pike's head appears from nowhere a split second before line sizzles from the reel and the fish tail-walks across the surface in a lather of foam. Or you could work the lure back virtually to your feet, only to have it wrenched away as you prepare to lift it up and into another cast. On another throw, you might wait for the disturbance to flatten off, and before you even start the retrieve up will come a pike and grab the plug when it is lying immobile.

I have in fact experienced something similar when presenting static deadbaits and using a red and white slider float well over depth completely flat on the surface. On several occasions, usually in the early morning long before the sun has risen, right out of the blue up has popped the head of a pike and grabbed the float simply lying there completely inert. I have always presumed, until it felt the wood or plastic against its teeth, that the pike simply mistook the flat float for a dead fish floating on the surface. And perhaps this is how they view the static plug.

One thing is certain, however. For imparting the most life-like action to surface plugs (and sub-surface lures), the best rod for the job is one with a snappy tip action (see p. 33). This is why the short, single-handed American bait-casting rods are so effective. Every single jerk and twitch is transferred to the artificial instead of being absorbed by the rod, as happens with soft-actioned, two-piece spinning rods.

With a surface lure, from the moment it touches the surface the retrieve should be as varied and as unusual as you can make it. Encourage it to gurgle by slamming the rod tip down to the surface. Jerk it, pause, twitch, gurgle again. Leave it static for a few seconds, jerk, twitch, pop, pause and so on. The variety of movements is as endless as the types of lures you can try. But be forever ready for that sudden hit by immediately whacking the rod back high to set the hooks and keep it high in a powerful curve, lest the pike's antics shake out the hooks. And for this it requires slack line. So play pike hard on artificials, giving line on demand, but begrudgingly.

BOAT-FISHING

Living in Norfolk has taught me one fundamental principle about pike fishing large stillwaters during the winter months. Going afloat allows so much water to be covered, resulting of course in many more pike in the net. There are, however, several important facts concerning boat-fishing that the newcomer might first like to consider before booking a dinghy for the day.

Firstly, as it is dangerous to erect an umbrella when in a small boat (or in any boat), you need to be well equipped with warm, waterproof clothing, plus hot drinks and snacks. Sitting on a hard, wooden seat for up to ten hours at a session is, to say the least, uncomfortable, so take along a padded waterproof tackle-box seat cushion. A square of thick foam covered in a bin liner will do at a pinch. To minimize noise upon bare floorboards, which is the easiest way of spooking pike (water is an extremely effective carrier of sound waves), and as a cushion upon which to lay pike for unhooking, I use a 6 ft long roll of ½ in thick dense foam sheeting. Old carpet underlay suffices nicely for this, as it does not absorb water.

Lastly, in terms of necessity, ensure that as well as a decent pair of oars the boat has a long rope at each end to which are tied heavy mudweights; not an improvised weight such as two house bricks tied together, or a piece of pig iron, but proper dense weights. There is nothing more frustrating, having contacted pike in rough weather, than to be suddenly blown away from the area because the

When the sun rises early, illuminating the cold water of winter, hectic sport on artificial lures can be expected. Andy Davison catches the pike of Rockland Broad in an aggressive mood.

mudweights are too light. Those which hold best in the strongest winds are small. The solid-steel mudweights provided with holiday cruisers are comparatively small, yet owing to their density hold the largest of boats in wind and even in strong river currents. However, steel weights are extremely expensive so why not make your own (which you can then take along and use wherever you hire a boat) by filling a couple of 2-gallon maggot buckets with concrete (fig. 33). To attach the rope bend a 10 in length of ¼ in mild steel into the shape shown so it protrudes from the bottom of the bucket when turned upside down on soft earth (make a narrow hole in the ground to take the wire), and fill with concrete to within 1 in of the lip. Within two days your mudweights will be ready for use after adding a suitable length of soft ½ in nylon rope to each at least twice the depth of anywhere you might fish.

As mentioned in the tackle chapter, echo-sounders are a great addition for locating the deepest areas of waters both large and small, but are not, I repeat not, a prerequisite for

Going afloat is the only way of exploring and coming to grips with big, wild waters. These pike fishermen prepare for a day on Loch Marlee in Perthshire, famous for its hard-fighting specimens.

catching pike. Their use can come later, when you have learnt the fundamentals of boat-fishing. The same can be said of outboard engines. Huge waters apart, you will learn to understand and be at one with pike fishing from an open dinghy far better by rowing quietly and positively, not aimlessly flitting from one area to another simply because getting there is easy with an engine.

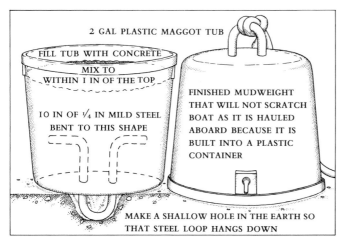

2 GAL PLASTIC MAGGOT TUB

FILL TUB WITH CONCRETE

MIX TO WITHIN 1 IN OF THE TOP

10 IN OF ¼ IN MILD STEEL BENT TO THIS SHAPE

FINISHED MUDWEIGHT THAT WILL NOT SCRATCH BOAT AS IT IS HAULED ABOARD BECAUSE IT IS BUILT INTO A PLASTIC CONTAINER

MAKE A SHALLOW HOLE IN THE EARTH SO THAT STEEL LOOP HANGS DOWN

FIGURE 33 *Making mudweights*

Wind strength and direction is perhaps the biggest single obstacle the boat fisherman has to overcome apart from choice of fishing partner. Make no mistake about it, some anglers never come to terms with fishing afloat. They are noisy, continually moaning about the weather or wanting to be on the move, and in some circumstances are downright dangerous the minute they leave terra firma. So whilst it is nice to share a cold day with a boat partner, choose someone whose idiosyncrasies are not going to drive you barmy after a couple of hours, and above all choose someone you can rely on.

In terms of technical application it helps to divide the boat up mentally into two equal parts so that each angler has his own corresponding area of water to fish, assuming that the weather permits an ideal mooring side-on to the wind. This takes a little extra time and care, but the results are so much better than rowing out and simply lowering the mudweights over the side, as fig. 34 illustrates.

Both anglers have an equal area to work and search, regardless of methods used, with an invisible line drawn across the middle of the boat and water. When the wind is too uncomfortable for a side-on anchorage, or when even the heaviest weights will not hold, it is advisable to anchor

FIGURE 34 *Anchoring side-on to the wind*

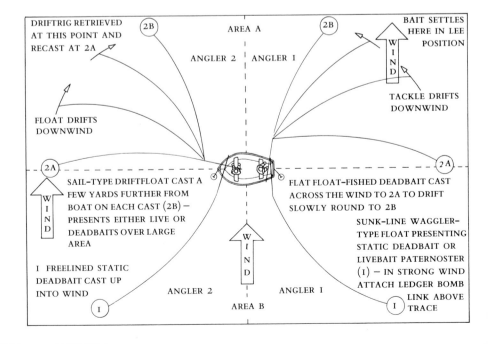

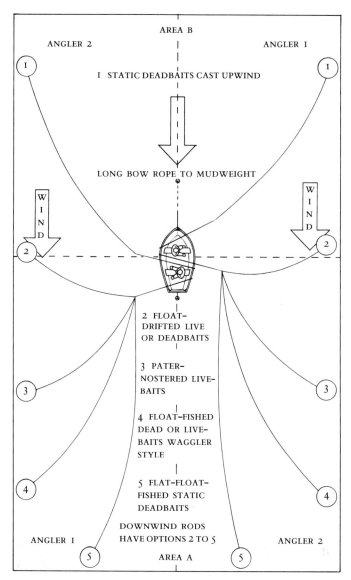

FIGURE 35 *Anchoring bows into the wind*

Within the figure:

AREA B

ANGLER 2   ANGLER I

I STATIC DEADBAITS CAST UPWIND

LONG BOW ROPE TO MUDWEIGHT

WIND

WIND

2 FLOAT–DRIFTED LIVE OR DEADBAITS

3 PATER–NOSTERED LIVE–BAITS

4 FLOAT–FISHED DEAD OR LIVE–BAITS WAGGLER STYLE

5 FLAT–FLOAT–FISHED STATIC DEADBAITS

DOWNWIND RODS HAVE OPTIONS 2 TO 5

ANGLER I   ANGLER 2

AREA A

bows into the wind (fig. 35). Start by lowering the bows mudweight and pay out at least twice the depth of rope so that whenever wave action lifts the bows, it does not bounce the mudweight (fig. 36A). Get it wrong (fig. 36B) and the boat will not hold position in strong winds. Once the long bows rope and mudweight are holding, put down the stern mudweight on a relatively short (steadying) rope. The imaginary dividing line between the anglers then runs down the length of the boat, through the middle from

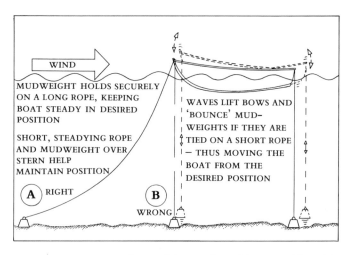

FIGURE 36 *Anchoring in strong winds*

bows to stern, so each can fish out from his own side with a full 180° to cover.

You will see from the diagrams (assuming two rods are used by each angler) that each also fishes across the water without affecting the other so long as the invisible line is adhered to. This is important because it maximizes the potential pike areas around the boat in a whole 360° circle, and provides a mental picture of the divisions within the area for experimenting with various techniques.

Remember when out afloat on a huge expanse of stillwater (unless you are fishing towards the shoreline up

No wonder Lee Wilson looks happy. Anchoring the boat bows into the wind and presenting static deadbaits both up and down wind, he has been able to cover a wide area, resulting in this fine fish.

against obvious pike-holding features like reed-beds and overhanging or sunken trees) that there is generally little indication of where the bait should best be placed other than depth. So if the bottom is of even depth over much of the fishery it pays to think in terms of taking a grid-searching approach with the emphasis on downwind, across wind and upwind areas in relation to the boat's anchorage.

This permits the use of virtually any method from the freelined static deadbait to drift-fishing livebaits or dead-baits. You simply use the most likely method on the day, or indeed a whole variety of methods throughout the day, until one is successful, considering weather and water conditions as you would if bank-fishing, and using the wind to full advantage.

For instance, consider area A in fig. 34, part of which being in the lee of the wind, can be fished effectively by Angler 1 with a greased line and 'sliding flat float rig' presenting a static deadbait on the bottom. What is more, by casting slightly across the wind and flicking off a belly of line downwind, the bait can even be drifted along the bottom for a while and worked into lee positions far in excess of distances that can be cast. Angler 2 could fish likewise or work his part of area A with either live or dead baits beneath a sail-type drift float (see p. 109), starting with short casts and working progressively further out after each drift. Both anglers could also wobble deadbaits or lure fish as alternative 'active' methods within area A.

Area B, which incorporates both across the wind and upwind options, is rarely used to full advantage by most pike fishermen because, unless the line is well sunk below the waves when float fishing, the bait is whisked away far too quickly downwind, resulting in both baits being ridiculously close to each other. This is hardly conducive to searching the entire area effectively. In this instance a waggler-type (bottom end) 'loaded slider rig' is perfect for presenting a static, bottom bait across the wind. In really gusty weather use an unloaded slider and add a bomb above the trace to nail the bait to the bottom. Angler 2 could fish his B area with a freelined static deadbait by casting it directly upwind. It is worth remembering always to pinch three or four swan shot on the trace immediately below the swivel so that drop-back runs can easily be detected. Without a float to create valuable slack the pike must feel a certain amount of resistance when sucking up a freelined static deadbait, steadied with swan shot, which is why they invariably belt off at speed directly away from the boat. Then again, it could be that the pike just happens to be working an upwind course when it locates the bait and simply carries on in that direction. Certainly this can be verified on those really windy days when most runs come to the upwind rod. Strangely, such occasions are far from uncommon, which prompts me to suggest that there is far more to the upwind phenomenon than meets the eye.

In really choppy weather with white horses topping the waves, for instance, when it becomes pertinent to anchor bows into the wind, I become more optimistic about the upwind baits being taken, even when casting range is greatly reduced. Incidentally, for maximum distance when pushing baits into a strong wind, the mackerel tail, due to its density, is hard to beat. Half an eel (the head end) casts well too.

Many past experiences spring to mind for illustrating the importance of placing the bait up into the wind. However, one particular occasion stands out because my boat partner at the time, Doug Allen, in just four casts to exactly the same spot within the space of half an hour, boated pike of 16, 17, 18 and then 19 lb. All took a static deadbait placed upwind from the boat not 25 yd out. In fact, wind strength inhibited any greater distance.

Now were these fish simply working through a particular route on the shallow broad we were fishing? Or were they lying huddled together in a tight group, attracted perhaps by a fodder fish shoal close by, with Doug's deadbait coincidentally plopped right on top of them? We had other baits lying quite close by to try and capitalize on the situation, but only from that tiny area did the action happen. And if I remember correctly those four pike late in the afternoon provided our only runs of the day. This prompts me to suggest that had we concentrated only upon presenting our baits downwind of the boat, we would have blanked totally.

There is no doubt that, once anchored, it pays dividends to present baits with varying methods within a grid and wind division basis. Think of the boat as your very own piece of bank in the middle of the lake, with the advantage of also having water behind in which to search, so your chances of pike are doubled.

When searching huge, even-depthed lakes, broads, meres or pits, there are days when in complete contrast to anchoring, fishing on the drift will produce numbers of pike. I much prefer mild weather for drifting because pike are generally more active and respond well to baits on the move, either wobbled deadbaits or artificial lures. The secret is to row well upwind to the very top of the fishery and to work back with the wind, working baits on both sides of the boat as it drifts slowly along. Manoeuvre the boat so it starts side-on to the wind and to ensure it remains that way for drifting at an acceptably slow rate, tie a keep-net behind the boat at each end to act as drogues.

Special boat drogues are available for fly fishing trout reservoirs where drifting is a popular technique because it covers so much water. So if you intend doing any amount of drift fishing, invest in a specialized drogue.

When a hot area is located, quickly lower the mudweights and explore the area exhaustively before continuing the drift. It is a wonderfully effective way of locating pike in vast areas of water that are completely bare of visible features. Obviously you can only wobble deadbaits or work artificial lures with the one rod, but there is nothing to stop you using a second, 'sleeping' outfit by trailing a deadbait behind the boat. This often takes pike that follow lures in but sheer away at the last moment. Try it and see.

River boat fishing

Boat-fishing in running water is virtually the same as in stillwater, except that current pace and direction must be taken into account. Rivers invariably contain very definite habitats and pike-holding features or areas, and because they are easier to read, you can quietly anchor to full advantage, spending say an hour or so in each likely spot before pulling the mudweights and drifting with the flow downstream to the next likely area.

So that each angler enjoys both up and downstream lies, consider the set-up in fig. 37, where the boat has been anchored bows-on to the flow, a rod's length out from one bank. Anchoring right in the middle is not only dangerous

From an anchorage at the end of a deep gully way out in the middle of a large gravel pit, and armed with a hi-tec Humminbird fish-finder plus enough lures to start a tackle shop, a pike fisherman works his end of the boat.

With both mud-weights on the bottom of the River Bure at Wroxham and within casting range of several boat dyke entrances, angling artist Chris Turnbull and his brother work livebaits and deadbaits when the river is un-usually quiet.

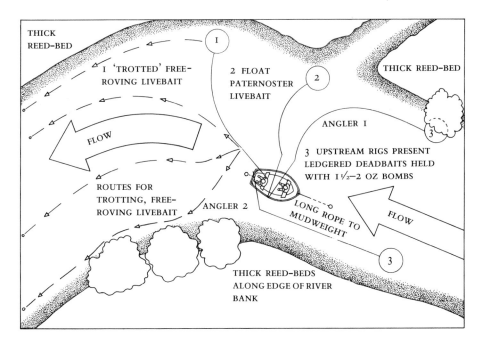

THICK REED-BED

1 'TROTTED' FREE-ROVING LIVEBAIT

2 FLOAT PATERNOSTER LIVEBAIT

THICK REED-BED

FLOW

ANGLER 1

3 UPSTREAM RIGS PRESENT LEDGERED DEADBAITS HELD WITH 1½–2 OZ BOMBS

ROUTES FOR TROTTING, FREE-ROVING LIVEBAIT

ANGLER 2

LONG ROPE TO MUDWEIGHT

FLOW

THICK REED-BEDS ALONG EDGE OF RIVER BANK

if other craft use the river regularly, it is invariably against the local river by-laws. Note that Angler 1 presents a ledgered deadbait on his upstream rod and a paternostered livebait on the downstream outfit, fished across the flow into the mouth of a confluence.

FIGURE 37 *Boat fishing on rivers*

Angler 2 also fishes a ledgered deadbait on his 'sleeping' outfit, presented with the bale arm open and a loop of line trapped beneath a strong run clip or elastic band over the handle, so only the pull of a pike and not the current can initiate a run. His downstream rod presents a float-fished, free-roaming livebait trotted 2 ft off bottom, along different lines, searching across the river thoroughly. As change methods, both anglers could swap their livebait rigs for wobbled baits, artificial lures, or even static deadbaits when the river colours up after heavy rain and pike switch to hunting more by smell than a combination of vibrations and sight. Playing the waiting game with four static deadbaits from the one boat is then the best approach.

Good pike fishing

INDEX